Introduction to the Tarot-Stones

Keith Ruch

Introduction to the Tarot-Stones

by

Keith Ruch

Second Edition

published by The Hermit's Grove

Editing:
Jana Horst, editor
Rev. Paul Beyerl, editor

Cover Photo:
Rev. Paul Beyerl

Introduction to the Tarot-Stones

published by:

The Hermit's Grove
16501 County 13
Houston, MN 55943

Dedicated to the four pillars of medicine:

Dedication to the Joy of Learning
A Knowledge of the Psychology of Astrology
Skill in Herbal Medicine and Alchemy
Commitment to a Virtuous Life

Front cover photo by Rev. Paul Beyerl

Library of Congress Control Number - 2014943273
ISBN 978-0-9655687-9-1

This edition published by The Hermit's Grove

Table of Contents

Chapter One: The Beginning

Prior to getting started, the aspirant is well advised to become aware of the characteristics of each stone. Study the color, shape, and size of each particular stone. Be sure to ponder the stones, feel the energy that surrounds them. Form a relationship with each stone, because they will be your guides along the path to greater comprehension and awareness.

The Tarot-Stones come individually arranged in a clear plastic bag to enable the aspirant to examine the stone's traits. The significant objective is to become aware of each stone as you would an individual person. This cannot be stressed enough, because it is an important element to the success of this endeavor. Try refraining from taking the stones out of the bags prematurely. Let's say that the stones were removed from their bags early, how would you know which stone was which? The knowledge eludes the fool and the stones' identities would be lost. Once you develop a better acquaintance with the stones feel free to remove them from their bags to cleanse them. Cleansing the stones could entail soaking them in water for a full lunar cycle. One could also place them in salt until all prior energies have been drained out leaving them clean and ready to use.

When using the Tarot-Stones, your intuition should be your guide along the Path. Do not let a gut feeling go unheeded, it is usually the right choice. Do not hesitate to tote the stones around with you when you go out. How does carrying a certain stone make you feel? Does that feeling change when you switch to another stone? If you feel compelled to replace an existing stone with one of higher worth then do so, but keep in mind that even though the top quality stones will have the same energies of the lower cost ones, the energies of the more expensive stones may be more potent. The choice is inevitably up to the aspirant's temperament.

Chapter Two: History of the System of the Tarot-Stones

It all started with a dream, which is now forgotten. I awoke from this dream with a vague notion of a "new" system of divination. Well, maybe not a "new" system per say , but more of a coupling together of two established systems; the tarot and stone lore. The God/Goddess gave me this system to share with you. With the support of Rev. Paul Beyerl; I have the pleasure of conveying it in this book. Five minutes after I awoke many thoughts of the system were running through my head. I happened to look up to see the waning quarter moon, the Moon Goddess in Her crone aspect. She then disappeared behind a bank of clouds for the night. Immediately following Her disappearance I thought, "What a wonderful gift the Goddess has given me this night; but how was I going to accomplish such a lofty goal; and why did the Goddess choose me to transfer this knowledge?"

Sitting down with pen in hand, I proceeded to go through the tarot cards writing what I felt the cards meant. With my Rider-Waite tarot deck, and a copy of Rev. Paul's book, The Symbols and Magick of Tarot, I began to work my way through the deck one card at a time. The first card I drew was the Queen of Pentacles. After writing commentary for seventeen of the cards I reread the words I wrote. Reading those pages astonished me. After I completed writing on the seventy-eight cards, I had around half a page of script for each card. Not so many words, but what was written was meaningful. It was the start of something good.

Utilizing Rev. Paul's book, Gem and Mineral Lore, I discerned which stone's energy matched which tarot card's meaning. In his book I found a wealth of information to guide me in my quest.

It is hoped that after you become familiar with this system of Divination, you will also find joy. If you receive a few sparks of knowledge or insight into the Mysteries, then I am overjoyed to be of service. Just touching the life of one person makes it all worth it. I have spent a great deal of time and energy producing this book and system of Divination, but I have gained insight into the Mysteries. I have learned enough from this adventure to know that the Mysteries will not lay themselves at the aspirant's feet. One must be willing to search the far reaches of the Universe to gain a glimpse into the Mysteries. Like the Fool, one has to be prepared to take the plunge into the abyss. To scale the escarpment, it is necessary to be sure-footed so you reach the top of the mountain safely. You may feel you have reached a pivotal point of achievement, but alas, the journey has just begun. One should be prepared to traverse the unknown to continue the greatest journey in the world; "LIFE."

Chapter Three: Introduction to the Spreads

There are so many types of spreads available to the aspirant today that I offer the two here only as examples. It is up to you to find those which fit your personality. What is important is that you feel that the spread is adequate.

The first layout calls for the aspirant to shake the bag of stones until you feel the action is sufficient. Proceed to draw one stone at a time. Lay the stone on a flat surface; whether on a special cloth or a piece of leather is up to you. Do not, however, lay the stones on a bare surface. I say this because the energies of the surface you lay them on might interfere with the energies of the stones. The stone's energies may be tainted with that of the surface, and would need to be re-cleansed. Be sure to have something handy to protect the stones. Personally, I find a fluffy cloth like fleece keeps the stones in place better.

The first stone pulled from the bag is called the "Significator Stone." This stone represents you, or the situation at hand.

The second stone is drawn and is placed directly under the Significator Stone. This position represents what was or what will become the past. It will tell the aspirant what the conditions of the inner self were.

The third stone is placed to the right of the second; this position depicts the present situation. It will provide a look at how your energies are reacting to the situation of the here and now.

The fourth stone is placed to the right of the third; this last position is an indicator of things to come. The fourth stone brings insight to the future of the inner self as it relates to the outer self. It tells of what needs to changed, or what needs to remain the same so your future self may gain from the experience.

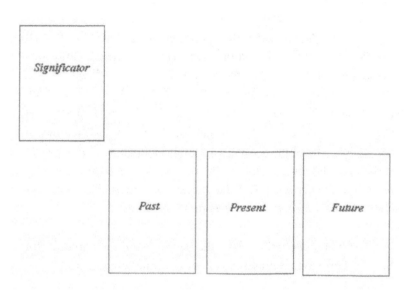

Another spread calls for the aspirant to take the first stone and place it on the surface you are working on; this is the Significator placement.

The second stone is drawn and arranged below the Significator; this represents the inner self and how it functions.

The third stone is placed beneath the Significator and second stone; this placement represents your goals, or your Highest Ideals in the situation.

The fourth stone is then sat down to the right of third stone; this position sheds light on the past as you journey into the present.

The fifth stone is selected and situated to the right of the second and above the fourth stone; this placement describes the family or the affairs of the family.

The sixth stone is set above the fifth and to the right of the Significator Stone; this represents the state of the aspirant's mind and body.

The seventh stone is then laid to the right of the Significator, and the sixth stone; this placement embodies one's religious outlook or the Path one is currently on.

The eighth stone is drawn and placed below the seventh stone and to the right of the fifth and second stones; this stone brings news of one's friends, if you are destined to make new friends or lose old ones.

The ninth and final stone is taken from the bag and is placed below the eighth stone and to the right of the third and fourth stones. This is the future or the final outcome of the situation. It is the end result of the reading.

Significator	6	7
2	5	8
3	4	9

Chapter Four: Introduction to the Major and Minor Arcana and the Stones

Greetings aspirant, I am here to guide you along the Path of Higher Spirituality. The Tarot-Stones will enhance knowledge of one's internal energies. As a spiritual being you inherently have energies within your aura. When you come in contact with other people and other sentient beings you share or swap energies.

You can use the Tarot-Stones to cleanse your internal energies. If you feel down in the dumps, or just a little off, it may be because your energy has been tainted. To cleanse one's energies there are many methods. One is to take a long hot shower, then pick a stone from the bag. You may wish to just pick one at random or choose one individually, it is up to you. Meditate on the stone's appearance at first, then as you move deeper into the stone's interior become aware of the energies in the stone. Imagine this energy washing over you, and washing away all that old, unwanted energy.

This chapter begins with the Major Arcana commentary followed by information on the The Fool to The World cards. Each card is followed by a stone. There are descriptions of the cards and stone's meanings. It is up to you to add your own feelings, insights, and interpretation.

Getting to know the stones will be very important. Keeping a journal will prove useful in this venture. A record of one's workings with the Tarot-Stones is important to follow your progress and make adjustments in your practice. A prior working knowledge of stone lore and the tarot is not necessary to begin, but would help considerably.

The Minor Arcana consist of fifty-eight cards or stones that consists of four suits: Swords, Wands, Cups, and Pentacles. Each suit starts with an Ace then progresses through the numbers up to ten followed by the court cards: Page, Knight, Queen, and King.

The Major Arcana are billboards that show you what is right and wrong in you life. They are there to alert you to things that might be unseen or otherwise overlooked.

The Minor Arcana are more like a subtle hint to things occurring in one's life. Even though they are called Minor Arcana, they are serious and should not be taken lightly. If there is a problem revealed in the reading by the appearance of the Minor Arcana, you may wish to review the Ace of that suit. When one is in search of the appropriate road to travel, look to the Ace of the Minor Arcana to find the Path once again. The Ace is the beginning, and will get you back on track. If you are still lost and confused you may wish to review all the stones of that suit to reevaluate the situation.

In this book you will find commentary on the Rider-Waite Tarot cards and Stone Lore. The Tarot-Stones are not meant to solve all your problems or fix life. They will not win you the lottery, but they can help to alleviate some of the stress from unwanted energies that are affecting one's life. It is wise to ever strive to be better today then you were yesterday. If you measure your success in years you are far better off. Ask yourself this, "Am I better today then I was a year ago?" If even just a little bit of a change was accomplished you have gained in the struggle of life.

By utilizing the Tarot-Stones it is possible for the aspirant to find themselves in tune with the latent energies that affect their lives. This is but the start of the a venture. You have decided to take the initiative and make a difference in your life. The Tarot-

Stones are not a complete system without your confidence and energy. Understanding the brief interpretations here is only one step toward the goal. It is you and your intuition that makes this system manifest.

Each stone has its own qualities and correspondences. Once you feel comfortable with your knowledge of the Tarot-Stones you may wish to perform readings for others. This would be a great idea because the more you do readings, the better acquainted you will become with the stones. However, if you are just now getting familiar with this system you are well advised to become acquainted with the stones and their meanings first. Achieving a basic connection to the energies of the stones is paramount to the success of this quest.

Do not forget to cleanse the stones either before or after each use. This is a very important action to do as it rids the stones of prior built up energies This will make the stones more receptive to the energies of the person receiving the reading.

After you cleanse the stones, pick one from the bag and observe its color, shape, and size. Take note of anything that stands out that can be an indication to the stone's identity. Write down your findings in your journal for future use. If you have not already done so, take another stone out of the bag. Feel the stone's energy; how does holding it make you feel? Is the feel of this stone different than the other? Try holding one in each hand; is there a difference in the energies? Can you feel the difference between the two? Try picking out several and see how their energies complement, or repel each other.

Do not forget to write down anything you might discover. Also remember to return the stones to their proper bags until you have a good understanding of the identities of the stones. Learning is an important part of following the Path to Greater Understanding.

Rock Healing Meditation.

Start by picking out a stone from the bag, or choose your favorite stone for healing. Cleanse the stone by soaking it in water with three equal measures of salt for at least an hour, the longer the better. This will "wash" away the impurities, and prepare the stone for your journey. After this action dry off the stone, if you wish, by using a clean if not consecrated towel. Try to use the same towel time after time, and it is better to hand wash it rather then tossing it in the washing machine. Hand washing allows your personal energies to permeate the towel.

After this action, place a pinch of Mugwort into a fire-proof receptacle. A sea shell works great for this part. Next place a pinch of sage on top of the Mugwort. Set it to flame. This is referred to as smudging. By allowing the smoke to pour over you and the stone, it purifies yourself, the stone, and the area around you as well. The smoke of the sage is purifying and banishes all negativity. The smoke from mugwort helps one to maintain a meditative state.

These actions introduce all four elements; Earth, Air, Fire, and Water. Now you have banished all negativities within the stone. When ready, get in a comfortable position and play your favorite soft music or sounds, and relax every muscle. Let all your troubles wash away and prepare to take a journey deep within the center of the stone.

Place the stone in your projective or dominant hand palm up, with fingers spread open all the way, but comfortably. Look at the stone, turn it around in your palm, and observe the stone's characteristics. Allow yourself to disappear into the stone. As you look at this ancient piece of Mother Earth know that She loves you dearly. Know that you are of the Earth, and you are Her child.

Now delve deep into the cracks and crevices to the very center of the stone's "heart." What Mysteries lie there to be uncovered? What secrets does this stone have hidden within its depths? Ask the stone any questions you wish or, if you are seeking healing, ask the stone to lend you healing energies. Follow the pathways of sediments and minerals to the exterior of the stone. When you reach the outer most perimeter of the stone, start to come out of your reprieve to the material world. You may want to carry this stone around with you to remain in contact with the energy of the stone. Should you be gathering energy for another, then it is better (but not always necessary) for them to have possession of the stone to receive the energy.

Chapter Five:The Major Arcana

O
The Fool
Uranus

Pyrite [Fool's Gold]

The Fool stands in utter bliss upon a precipice. You have travelled far. The Fool holds in one hand a single rose; not the red rose of love, not the yellow rose of friendship, not even the black rose of death, but the white rose of perfection. The Fool's faithful companion is happy to be at the end of the journey and jumps for joy at the thought of reaching the culmination of their travels. It seems the Fool can go no further, however, the mountains loom in the background awaiting the aspirant to scale the heights. This may be a sign of failed hopes, but the journey does not cease. The aspirant must take that plunge into the abyss to summit the mountain where the hermit awaits. Have you embraced the disciplines of faith? Are you ready to dive into the great unknown? This card shows that lessons were gained for a greater understanding of life. The trials are past, and you must look forward to a brighter rainbow. This has been a test of endurance. The aspirant may fall more than once, and get hurt. You have to take it in stride, get back up, and move forward. Dwelling on the past will only bring heartache. Though you may learn from prior events, do not brood on them. Put aside negative experiences, live for today, and dream of tomorrow.

Pyrite

The Pyrite stone is attributed to the Fool card. Pyrite is also known as Fool's Gold by some. Pyrite may glitter like gold, but one must not allow Pyrite to fool you into false hopes. Pyrite is a fabulous stone to meditate upon; its deep crevices takes you on a journey into the depths of understanding. Pyrite is thought to allow the possessor to send and receive telepathic communications with another who possesses a Pyrite stone. When a Pyrite stone enters a reading it is advising the aspirant to contemplate one's actions. Is the aspirant being foolish, hasty, or rash? This stone brings a warning to stay away from pitfalls. Make a retreat into the spiritual by meditating on this stone; there is a lesson to be learned from this experience. Do not be foolish at this time; the higher summit awaits the wise aspirant. Do not step off into the the unknown without first realizing what awaits the Fool. The aspirant is well advised to keep on the Path, to the road that leads to greater understanding. When carried, Pyrite lends its energies to guide the aspirant to the top of the mountain. Pyrite helps communication between loved ones.

I
The Magician
Mercury

Clear Quartz Crystal

The aspirant is seen here with all the tools needed to practice the craft; Swords (Air), Wands (Fire), Cups (Water), and Pentacles, (Earth). Around the Magician's waist are the cords of initiation. The infinity sign above the magician's head is worn as if it is a crown of achievement. In the aspirant's one hand is a wand pointed downward, in the other there is a wand pointed upward. This is reminiscent of the Hermetic Principle: "As above, So below." The aspirant must seek the balance of the Hermetic Principle to obtain the knowledge the world has to offer. The flowers speak of the love and fertility of the Mother. You have what it takes to perform the rituals of the Magician at hand. You may obtain this Truth by first learning the lessons being taught by the Universe. What lessons come after one has reached the heights of spirituality? You must continue along the Path for there is much more to learn, there is farther to travel. Staying on the Path will enable you to complete the journey. When one reaches the summit of the mountain and becomes the Hermit, you must remember that even this is not the end of the quest. The mountain's top is not the beginning nor the end. Spirituality and well-being are but two of the reasons to search the far reaches of the Universe to find what you seek. One who understands the Great Mystery will be at total peace with the Universe.

Clear Quartz Crystal

Clear Quartz Crystal is attributed to the Magician. Quartz has been used for such things as wands, crystal balls, staves, and magickal jewelry. Quartz aids in magick, healing, and spirituality. It is a great stone to use in meditation. This stone can also be used to divine dreams. When sleeping with this stone under your pillow one will have more vivid dreams and it will be easer to learn more of your dream's meaning. Carry a Quartz Crystal around with you in a pocket, purse, or in a bag around your neck to bring its magickal properties into your life. When the Quartz Crystal is pulled in a reading it is telling the aspirant that magick is afoot. To utilize this magickal energy remember to ground and center to stay balanced in life.

II
The High Priestess
The Moon

Shell

The aspirant is presented here as the High Priestess; a symbol of great reward and spiritual gain. The High Priestess has traveled a long way to get to where she is; she has learned much in her youth and has gained wisdom since her childhood. The High Priestess wears the Triple Moon Crown of achievement and the pomegranates behind her symbolize fertility. She wears the symbol of Christianity around her neck and she holds what looks like the Torah on her lap. This creates the perfect balance of the religions. The High Priestess challenges the aspirant to accept the views of others and to reserve judgement. The aspirant would be wise to learn from the High Priestess; as when goals in life have been accomplished, but you realize there is still more to gain. When Mysteries of the Universe have been revealed, yet you have advanced deeper into the unknown. When one seeks answers, but finds them naught, it is within that the answer lies.

Shell
Shell is attributed to the High Priestess. Shell lends its energies to unite the home in a domestic sense. If the Shell comes up in a reading it may be alerting you to something amiss in the home. Shell may be showing the aspirant that there is a need to reevaluate their hopes and wishes. What is it you really want in life? Shell will bring balancing energies to those who

listen to the voice of the ocean. She will speak to the listener during meditation; sometimes softly and other times loud. Remember that the Sea is wise, so listen carefully. Use the energies of Shell as the High Priestess would; weave the magick into your life. When Shell appears in a reading it is to keep your spirituality in balance.

III
The Empress
Venus

Emerald

The Empress sits upon a throne of soft cushions amongst wheat fields and trees. She wears a ritual necklace and a crown of six pointed stars; these symbolize the Mysteries of the Universe. The Empress appears to be young, her journey has just begun. No mountains are visible, but the river in the background flows down in a waterfall. The forest is lush, and the wheat is plentiful. The Empress wears a robe with pomegranates, a sign of fertility. The Venus symbol on the cushion at her feet speaks of female Mysteries and beauty. You sit upon the cushioned chair, and have the beautiful gifts of Mother Nature around you. The Mother of Nature calls you into action. You have gained in your pursuits, but you must move forward on the Path. Higher understanding awaits those who choose to seek it. The aspirant can achieve great knowledge from the Empress. There are lessons to be learned with this card. To gain the sheltered stature of the Empress one must use the material gains of the everyday life in moderation. The chair may be comfortable to sit upon, but it is up to you to gather the strength to climb the mountain's heights to achieve your goals.

Emerald

The Emerald is attributed to the Empress card. Emeralds have the power to detect lies. When an Emerald appears in a layout it suggests that someone may be lying to you or about you. The Emerald brings energies that can change things around in the possessor's favor. Emeralds are balancing and calming, and when submerged in one's bath water they help to alleviate stress, enabling you to make more refined decisions. The Emerald is used to heighten one's intuition on the matters that lay before you. Do not be afraid to follow that intuition. The Empress is calling you to come forward and be fruitful, do not waste time being pulled down by others. An Emerald carried on the person or meditated upon will help lend extra energy in order to heal one's self, maintain equilibrium, and calm the inner self so that you may become more aware of your surroundings.

IV
The Emperor
Aries

Ruby

The Emperor holds his scepter in one hand, reminiscent of the male and female polarities with the length of the scepter being the male aspect and the loop at the top being the female aspect. In the other hand is a globe, the sphere of energy or crystal ball to scry the future. The mountains in the background are rugged and steep. The Emperor himself has scaled those mountains and now he sits on his stone throne with its squared off corners. The Emperor does not look comfortable at all in his armored boots and chain mail shirt. He appears to be preparing for battle, or perhaps his battle has already begun. Four ram heads are upon his throne and there is a river flowing from the contours of the jagged cliff. Whether the battle one is currently having is physical, mental, emotional, or you are dealing with a habit or addiction, always keep pure your Highest Ideals. If you wish to conquer this battle, then it would be wise to stay on the right Path. One must strive to climb the cliff's rugged face to overcome this time of trial. The mountain top awaits the wise one who wishes to conquer their fears. There may be some hard lessons to learn with this card, but the rewards will be all the sweeter; persevere and you will make it to the summit safe and sound.

Ruby

Having the ability to hold the energies of both male and female polarities, the Ruby is attributed to the Emperor card. The Ruby is a passionate stone and allows the possessor to tap into the passions and emotions of others. When a Ruby shows up in a reading you may be seeing the fiery side of a relationship in the near future. To bring fire into a relationship allow yourself to be passionate, and willing to express your needs to the one you love. Carrying a Ruby can bring great success in love and money. Try meditating with a Ruby to help to alleviate the pain of battle. Rubies can help to ease conflict and stress in an argument, especially with loved ones. When conflict arises try to use a little compassion at those times. Carrying a Ruby will help ward off sickness and disease as well as sadness and despair. Therefore, if you are fighting a habit or addiction the Ruby would be a good stone to turn to. Ruby will lend its energies to bring insight to the inner self. A person wearing a Ruby with ill intentions are subject to their own malevolence. The aspirant can take the role of the Emperor, but must use his power wisely; misuse of that power can be harmful and detrimental to one's well-being. When a Ruby appears in a layout, it is warning the aspirant of conflict. This quarrel is usually with a loved one, so use the energy of a Ruby to help alleviate the tension between the two of you during those times of trouble.

V
The Hierophant
Taurus

Carnelian

The aspirant has achieved great stature in the world, as well as the spiritual heights one has longed for, now you are the Hierophant. The Hierophant has all the tools needed to conduct the religious rites. The aspirant should remember at this time that with power and stature one must temper the ego; it is the wise aspirant who does not take for granted this position. The two pillars call for a need for balance. The aspirant is being watched by the congregation to determine if you have what it takes to accomplish what needs to be achieved. The Hierophant has been elevated to a high state of spirituality. One should always be mindful of their actions; others are watching. The aspirant has to learn from this experience. To stay at this level of spirituality one must keep the emotional state in check. The congregation is there to help support the Hierophant. One must be in control, and be willing to help in return.

Carnelian

Carnelian has been attributed to the Hierophant card. Carnelian brings in the masculine energies of the Divine while balancing the feminine energies of the Universe in a positive way. Carrying or meditating upon this stone will bring you closer to the Sun God and will also help to utilize the energies that allow the aspirant to move closer to the positive goal in their lives. Meditation upon this stone during ritual will help strengthen the spiritual discipline of the student. It will also improve one's concentration to remain focused. When Carnelian appears in a a reading it shows that the aspirant has an increased amount of joy in life. It has the power to bring the "here and now" to light. Maybe the time has come to focus attentions on one's family or to enjoy being with the one you love; be sure to take the time out of your busy schedule to take a breath and be thankful for the things that you have.

VI
The Lovers
Gemini

Pink Tourmaline

This card depicts a scene reminiscent of the Adam and Eve story. The angle above is a symbol of Divine inspiration. Is the angle above reprimanding the two for what they done or is the angle their relationship as they go through life? The polarities, male and female, stand as the two pillars and the trees, one in bloom, the o may also represent the pillars of the polarities. The tree is a symbol of knowledge. The mountains that stand between the two presents the Middle Pillar. It may be a reminder that spirituality is a pivotal point between man and women as lovers and the need to seek spirituality will serve to heighten their bond of love. The aspirant would be wise to learn the lessons from these two lovers, to be able to have Perfect Love and Perfect Trust one must be willing to stand naked before the Divine, revealing their whole selves and hiding nothing. The nakedness of the couple is a symbol of purity and innocence. To be purely innocent, one must strip themselves of the mundane burdens of the world, then only with pure intentions and peace in the heart can one stand before the Great Divine in love and respect.

Pink Tourmaline

Pink Tourmaline is attributed to the Loves card. Pink Tourmaline carries the virtue of unconditional love. When this stone appears in a reading it does not absolutely mean that you will find romantic love, it could be the love of a friend, or a reunion with the lost relationship. Carrying one of these stones will help to open the mind up to an unknown love. Since this stone lends its energies to calm fears and panic attacks. You could benefit by meditating upon this stone. Keep your intentions in mind while meditation to instill the stone with your essence. The Moss Agate leads you down the road of Perfect Love and Perfect Trust by understanding your roll in the relationship. Look into the stone, travel deep into its inner core. Feel the unconditional love of the Divine.

VII
The Chariot
Cancer

Lapis Lazuli

The Chariot driver who is dressed like a warrior and holds a pointed rod in one hand. The Chariot is seen leaving the city perhaps going to the battlefield. Above the drivers head is the eight-pointed star and on the shield are crescent moons with faces on them, a sure sign of the Moon Goddess's presence. The parities are present with the black and white, male and female sphinxes; the two pillars of dark and light. The two wheels of the chariot are also symbols of the two pillars with driver as the Middle Pillar. This card speaks of travel and getting away from the hustle and bustle of the city. The Chariot is going away from the watery abyss. Are you moving into battle or retreating from it? Pay heed to the Chariot driver's message; one must move into action so that you can achieve your goals in life; there may be battles of face, but remember that you can achieve great accomplishments when you win the battles. There may be scarring, but those scars will only make you stronger.

Lapis Lazuli

Lapis Lazuli is attributed to the Chariot card. This stone has a long history with humans, the ancient Egyptians used it extensively. When Lapis Lazuli appears in a layout it may be telling the aspirant that a journey is ahead or that balance has finally been achieved. This stone will lend strength to the mind and will enable one to complete a mental goal. Meditating upon a Lapis Lazuli will help alleviate depression, melancholy, and may be the key to settling down and focusing on a goal. It will also help increase spiritual wisdom to guide you along the Path. Lapis Lazuli has many attributes such as the ability to promote change and to lend an extensive level of awareness to the student. Lapis Lazuli can also assist in attaining the aspirants's Highest Ideals.

VIII
Justice
Libra

Moss Agate

Justice is seen here wielding a large sword with great strength and skill. Justice sits between the tow pillars, and as the Middle Pillar, casting judgement fairly and without emotional hindrance. Justice does not sit on a big plush, decorated throne, only a simple bench. The aspirant must keep in mind that Justice can only stay in this position when one makes the sacrifice of ones emotions to be impartial. The aspirant must sacrifice the material to keep from wanting more. One needs to sacrifice the ego for the good of both sides of the scale. You can take into account that you are in control of the situation. You must keep Perfect Balance to remain just. This may be a call to make adjustments to ones own way of thinking before you continue on the Path of life. To judge others is to be judged by others; watch how you judge, do not judge unfairly least you taste your own medicine.

Moss Agate

Moss Agate has been attributed to the Justice card. When studying this stone, keep in mind hat the Moss Agate appears in a reading when the aspirant has come to a pivotal point in your life and now judgement is at hand. The Moss Agate is a great stone to contemplate in this circumstance. This stone will help to keep you balanced, grounded, and centered. The Moss Agate can lend energy to heal the emotional hurts, and open the door to opportunity This is not the end of the road, it is just a speed bump or a hurdle to get over. Do not tarry too long or you may miss the grander things in life.When the Moss Agate shows up in a reading it is usually to tell you that the wrong doings need to be addressed, just keep in mind that there is a light at the end of the tunnel. At the top of the mountain the Hermit awaits the aspirant who takes the scales and balances them.

IX
The Hermit
Virgo

Jade

In this card the Hermit has reached the height of the mountain and shines the light for all to see and follow. The Hermit is wise and has traveled far and wide to reach this pinnacle of achievement. What is left after such a grand accomplishment? After all, one has reached the mountain 'ssummit. The Hermit, now the teacher, shines the light for the aspirant to follow, but it is only those who are destined to traverse the mountain's treacherous slopes that may see the light for what it truly is, "Divine Inspiration." The Hermit is resting from the journey. The aspirant is reminded that although the road to the top of the mountain seems to have come to the end, the journey is far from over; life goes on. The lessons of this card have brought you thus far; but now you must learn yet another lesson: be the beacon of light, shine bright, and do not let your ego get in the way. The aspirant would be wise to become one with the Hermit; to learn to teach, and teach to learn.

Jade

Jade is attributed to the Hermit card. A Jade stone is used to enhance spiritual well being. Jade allows you to journey to the heights of spiritual discipline. Shine your light on those who seek, and that light shines just as brightly back on you. When reflecting upon this stone, remember the Hermetic Principle, "As above, so below". Jade lends its energies to this endeavor. Jade is known for repelling negative emotions and gives a sense of peace and tranquility. When Jade shows up in a reading; it is an indication that the soul is at peace, the emotions are balanced, and things are progressing for the aspirant. If things are not going as you wish them to, perhaps one needs to embrace the disciplines of this stone to mend the hurt. Only when the aspirant is in Perfect Balance will the mysteries be unfolded. The wise aspirant will strive to obtain the position of the Hermit atop the mountain.

X
The Wheel of Fortune
Jupiter

Malachite

The elements are all present in the corners of this card. Each one is studying a book; the aspirant is advised to keep to their studies. As the wheel turns, the sphinx holds the Sword of Truth while sitting atop the wheel. A dog like creature (perhaps Anubis) lies lazily upon the wheel, and the yellow snake observes what is going around. The eight letters, written on the outer rim of the wheel speak of mysteries. One should seek to be in the middle of the wheel to discern what is occurring in the big picture. Keep in mind that the center of the wheel is more steady than the outer rim. Remember the words of the Great Mother in the Charge of the Goddess, "Keep pure your Highest Ideals, let naught stop you nor turn you aside." The Goddess speaks clearly, and the wise aspirant would listen to Her words.

Malachite

Malachite has been connected to the Wheel of Fortune card. Associated with the element of Earth, Malachite could represent the spinning of the planet. The aspirant has the power to steady the wheel; grounding is key to slowing or maybe even stopping the wheel so you can comprehend the Mysteries. A piece of this stone will protect the wearer from negative forces such as malevolent spirits, and from attacks of venomous creatures. Meditating upon this stone may give visions to those seeking to be at one with the Universe. Malachite may also be carried to tip the Wheel of Fortune in one's favor to become more prosperous, abundant, or keep one in good health. This stone may appear in a reading when things are about to change. Be prepared and do not forget to center yourself inside the wheel so you can cope with the challenges that you may be facing. To spin the Wheel of Fortune is to take a chance. If you are prepared to reap the rewards you must also be ready to handle the losses as well.

XI
Strength
Leo

Peridot

This lady has shown Perfect Love and Perfect Trust symbolized in the Infinity symbol above her head. The Lady brings strength to the seeker. She teaches that even the most ferocious beast can be tamed. Do not judge by appearances, they can be deceiving. To attain the achievement of Strength, embrace your fears to gain love and trust. It is amazing how many people fail to attain success because they are afraid of failure. When you build strength of character your goals can be achieved. Love tempers the ego, love strengthens the heart, and love attracts love. These lessons should not be difficult to understand. When you face challenges head on, you create a fulfilling life. Life is a beautiful gift, do not waste it on self-pity, instead have the strength to enhance your mind, body and spirit.

Peridot

Peridot is associated with the Strength card. Peridot lends energies and allows you to reach your full potential. This stone is warm and friendly and shows that Strength and the Lion can overcome the nature of the beast. Peridot can help to increase one's personal power and self worth. Meditate upon this stone to get an extra boost of energy. In a reading, Peridot may indicate the meeting of two souls, there is a possibility of romance. Carry a Peridot to shed negative emotions and behaviors to reveal your inner light. Peridot helps to achieve a greater understanding of yourself and obtain happiness in your life. Accordingly, this stone calms the nervous system; it reduces stress and helps resolve emotional tension. When Peridot is pulled in a reading it is a signal that the ego needs to be tamed. Let go of the inner beast, and let go of the primal instinct. Have the strength to carry on in Perfect Love and Perfect Trust. Discard whatever you fear, and release your stress.

XII
The Hanged Man
Neptune

Aquamarine

A man hangs suspended from the tree of wisdom; this tree is teeming with life. This tree offers guidance from birth, throughout life, continuing on through death, then begins again at rebirth. The point of hanging upside down is to gain insight into what was not previously perceived. The Hanged Man is in the Yoga position, with one leg crossing over the other in a figure-four. This represents each of the Four Directions, the Elements of Life, the Winds, and Archangels. Strive to learn what lessons the Divine has set before you. Meditating for too long can lead to dreaming, and excessive dreaming leads to false hopes and expectations. Do not hide in the ethereal world. Come out of your reprieve to experience life, because knowledge is incomplete without experience.

Aquamarine

Aquamarine is attributed to the Hanged Man. In many ways Aquamarine helps to achieve greater heights of understanding. While studying this stone be mindful that every human is imperfect and should strive to better the mind, body, and spirit.

Aquamarine lends healing energy to those who need it. This stone enhances ones ability to think clearly. This is an important aspect when meditating upside down in a tree. When an Aquamarine appears in a reading it indicates the need to meditate to enhance spiritual understanding. Do not procrastinate, things will get worse with time; seize the moment and take charge. Suspend your everyday life for spiritual enlightenment. Aquamarine is associated with the Element of Water. Water moves with fluid motions; it is illusive and flowing. Dreams and emotions resemble water; they ebb and flow. They react to the slightest disruption like a rock tossed into a still pool of water. Emotions can be a tricky thing to deal with; sometimes they are unbearable and at other times they are tranquil. An Aquamarine helps alleviate the unbalance in one's emotions, ease heartache, and gain equilibrium to pursue your Highest Ideals.

XIII
Death
Scorpio

Jet

Death sits astride his faithful steed coming to claim the soul of the deceased. Even in death there is life, as seen in the flowers in the maiden's hair, and in the child's hand. The sun rises between the two towers, the two pillars; with the sun as the Middle Pillar. The sailboat represents commerce; it does not hold still for anything. We see the Hierophant praying over the shell of the departed. The child holds a horn, perhaps to be used to herald Death to come collect the fallen. The young lady looks upset at the loss. Though this is a time filled with heartache and sorrow, there are indications of continuation. There is light on the horizon. You are reminded that you are not necessarily going to die a mortal death; it is most likely a symbolic death where the old dies out and the new is reborn. The life after death is more important than death itself. No matter what death holds; whether it is a new body or ego, life goes on.

Jet

Jet has been corresponded with the Death card. Jet lends its energies to help alleviate pain of emotional loss and helps those who deal with depression; Jet is also good for maintaining balance. One school of thought is that Jet repels negative energies, while another says that it absorbs negative energies; either way it is an excellent stone to wear or carry around. One is advised to contemplate what this death is, and how it affects them. This death does not necessarily mean the death of a loved one or the physical death of the aspirant. It does, however, remind you that there is need to look toward the horizon. The sun is shining, a new day is dawning, and you have a new chance at life. This death is not the end, but rather a new beginning. Jet can also help alleviate emotional storms when one feels like they have died inside. Meditation on this stone can help find future problems and locate the source of the issue. Only when you find the primary source of the negative influence can the healing commence. If negative energies are affecting you, use this stone to repel, or absorb them.

XIV
Temperance
Sagittarius

Azurite

Temperance stands with one foot upon the sturdy earth and the other dipping into the waters of emotions. Temperance holds two chalices and water is divided between the two of them into equal parts. The sun is rising on the horizon. The day dawns and your emotions are in balance. The daffodils behind temperance symbolize that spring is on its way. Spring is a time of new growth and new life. The triangle upon Temperance's robe is at the heart chakra. Temperance brings the kind of joy that leads one to great emotional rewards. Walk the well worn Path to reach the spiritual heights where the sun brightens the dark recesses of the emotions. The lessons of this card help one to obtain the aspirations of perfect balance. Keep treading water for you will soon be able to regain equilibrium. The emotions are tossed around at this time like a boat in a storm. To regain balance one can revert to the spiritual journey. If Temperance appears in a reading, do not fret - you have weathered the storm and now it is time to heal. Emotions may be rocky at times, not unlike a roller coaster ride that goes up and down.

Azurite

Azurite has been associated with Temperance. Azurite brings spiritual balance to mundane lives. This stone may be used in meditation practice to better understand the subconscious mind, and evolve one's mental growth. When an azurite shows up in a reading it is guiding you in your spiritual well-being. With one foot on the earth (material) and the other in the water (emotional), the aspirant needs to keep the balance of both. Meditating upon Azurite may increase the ability to perform self-hypnosis. When Azurite is carried it lends energies to comprehend what is happening around you. Azurite enables you to gather your senses so you may find the way to balance the emotions. Azurite's meaning in the reading will reveal an emotional unbalance in your life. To counteract the imbalance of emotions, you may wish to review other stones to see which one might help in this predicament.

XV
The Devil
Capricorn

Black Onyx

The aspirant has been bound with chains to pillars of this devil. This is a scary card to some, but it may be depicting a totally different set of circumstances to find a solution to the problem. To free one's self from this dismal fate, all one has to do is loosen the shackles around their neck; for this to be accomplished the aspirant must be ready to be freed. The woman in this card has the grapes at the end of her "tail" which represents fertility. The man in this card has fire at the end of his "tail", this represents the heat of desire. This card reminds the aspirant that some people may try to chain you to pillars of pain and suffering, but it is within your power to slip off those chains. No one else can do it for you. Make the choice to be free from the imprisonment of your own design. By allowing yourself to show love and compassion, you can break the chains and remove them.

Black onyx

Black Onyx is attributed to the devil card. Black Onyx can hold darkness within it, a belief which dates to old folk stories about spirits that were trapped within the stone and liked to visit and bring trouble to humans. More recently, however, people have started to believe that this stone brings protection rather than harm to the one holding it. When the Black Onyx appears in a reading do not fret over the fact that it is associated with the Devil card. The Onyx stone gives strength to endure in times of trouble. Though its appearance in a reading is a sign that something is amiss in the life of the aspirant, carrying an Onyx will strengthen you and enable you to tackle troubles, allowing life to move forward. This may be a test of your commitment to the spiritual well-being of your soul; when the Devil shows his face, smite him and send him packing. Onyx will attract energy into itself so be careful of what this stone comes into contact with. Do not forget to cleanse your Onyx. To keep this stone extra protected from outside influences, it is suggested that you place the stone in sage to keep it safe.

XVI
The Tower
Mars

African Bloodstone

When first encountered, the Tower seems like a dreadful sight of fire, smoke, and lightning, with people falling out of windows into the abyss. You may be asking yourself what good could come of this card. Remember that the Tower brings a warning that your life may be off track. You may be going through a moment of turmoil and need to get back on your feet. Pay heed to the fundamentals of life. By keeping your spirits light, and finding refuge in a friend's company, you will be able to regain the equilibrium you had prior to this fiasco. Meditation on the healing of mind, body, heart, and soul will aid in the stabilization of one's life. Stop what you are doing and regain a foot hold on life; this situation may seem out of control at the moment, but things will subside. Asking the Great Divine for assistance with the healing process will help tremendously. if you let things keep going out of control you will find that you are on a roller coaster ride, and you can not stop.

African Bloodstone

The African Bloodstone is attributed to the Tower card. Where the Tower card shows despair, tragedy, and calamity, the Bloodstone brings energies to counter the affects of the mishap. Carrying a Bloodstone will enhance the possessors' courage, logic, and wisdom, as well as give the carrier protection. Meditating upon this stone can bring insight to the elusive dreams of the future. This stone will help guide those who give counsel to make better choices. When African Bloodstone appears in a reading it is to alert the aspirant that something tragic may occur soon. Be mindful of the changes happening around you. The Tower being struck by lightning is a strong indication of a storm coming. Whether that storm is emotional, physical, or the actual weather remains to be seen. To counter the forces of negativity, carry a bloodstone. This stone will alleviate the stress of a situation. Listen to your dreams. What does your intuition tell you? Do not be afraid to let your gut feeling lead the way. Bloodstone lends the energy to alleviate heartache, hatred, and anger in the people around you. When a Bloodstone appears in a reading, do not hesitate to carry it around with you for a while to bring your dreams to life. Meditation on this stone can relieve some of the stress of the storm.

XVII
The Star
Aquarius

Amethyst

The Lady of the Heavens pours forth abundance of emotional and material wealth. One foot is planted on solid ground while the other is upon rippling waters. Eight pointed stars fill the sky as a bird watches intently from the branch of a tree. The birds feathers are ruffled; is it about to take off, or has it just landed? The bird is a messenger; look for correspondence soon. The aspirant is seen here beneath the starry night to gain emotional stability. You are better off to empty out your chalice of emotions to be filled with Divine inspiration. You may realize that to reach the mountain's top, you must use your intuition. The negative emotions need to be drained to make room for the positive ones.call upon Star to come and fill you with love, happiness, and kindness. If you feel lonely at night, try looking to the stars. The sky can bring you comfort in your darkest times. Feel the love of the sky, see the Moon Goddess gliding across the stark black background, and know that She loves you.

Amethyst

The Amethyst stone has been assigned to the Star card. Amethyst is calming and brings the aspirant tranquility. When an Amethyst appears in a layout, it is to herald that good things are coming; keep this stone close and utilize its energies. When meditating on an Amethyst, keep in mind these virtues; beauty, serenity, fulfillment, humility, love, perfection, piety, sincerity, spiritual balance, tranquility, and wisdom. This is an all around positive stone that can be used to calm mental disorders such as depression and melancholy. To fully comprehend workings of this stone it would be best for the aspirant to incorporate it into their everyday lives to see how it affects the energies that surrounds your daily life. Amethyst holds many positive qualities, do not hesitate to tap into them. When an Amethyst shows up in a layout represents a positive outlook for the aspirant. The Amethyst is a favorable stone to have in a reading because, it brings good, happy times. If you get an Amethyst in your spread it may be reminding you to utilize the virtues of this stone.

XVIII
The Moon
Pisces

Rainbow Moonstone

In this card the lobster comes out of the abyss the try and drag the aspirant to the depths of deceit and delusion. The dogs howl to the Moon Goddess in unrestful joy. The pillars are seen here to represent the dark and light. The Moon can be deceiving at times. The Moon pulls at the emotions especially when She is full. One may feel out of sorts and restless at the moment. To sooth the turmoil within, try meditating in a warm bath or shower. Rinse off the daily grime and let the water cleanse you through and through. Let your emotions be cleansed as well. The Moon card Is an interesting card to pull, it shows that something is just not as it seems. If you meditate long enough you will understand what is wrong and what to do about to. The Moon Goddess can entice you to be creative in many ways, That is possibly why so many people get into trouble on the Full Moon.

Rainbow Moonstone

Rainbow Moonstone has been ascribed to the Moon card. The Moonstone brings protection to those who are on a journey. In this case, it is a spiritual journey. This stone lends many virtues, such as wealth, love, wisdom, health, strength, and will. Keep in mind that sometimes this stone will amplify dark energies and draw negative people to you; to expel these energies meditate on this stone to find the underlying cause of the problem. In other words, do not carry this stone around with you if you are feeling negative yourself, for it will heighten this trait. Try another stone to counter the negative emotions at these times. Carrying a Moonstone when on a journey, especially one of a spiritual nature, will enable the wearer to focus on their duties to the community. Moonstone may also be utilized to scry dreams and to look toward the future. When a Moonstone appears in layout, it is usually indicating that a bump in the Path has slowed your advancement,inhibiting you from traveling any further; someone or something may be holding you back. The mountains of spirituality awaits those who are willing to scale the heights. You need only to put forth the effort, and place one foot in front of the other to reach the intended goal.

XIX

The Sun
Sun

Sunstone

A child sits astride a gallant white horse holding the The sun is in its full glory, and the flowers look lovingly at the child. This symbology resembles stories of purity and innocence. Is the wall behind the child an impediment, or is it the wall to a city? The aspirant is has a good standing spiritually, mentally, and physically. The sun is shining and the aspirant is naked of cares. Things are looking up for you, there are no mountains to scale at this time. This is a time of rest and relaxation, but do not forget that too much of a good thing is not always a good thing.Remember to enjoy life in moderation. Even in this time of tranquility there are lessons to be learned. Over-indulging in life's treasures can make you burn out, and become unbalanced. Too much time in the sun will eventually burn you.

Sunstone

Sunstone has been corresponded to the Sun card. Warm, loving, and the giver of life, the sun can hurt us, but we can not live without its heat and light. The plants thrive because of the sun's light. When carrying a Sunstone the warmth of the sun brings fertility to grow the ideas of the aspirant into fruition. Sunstone can be energizing so carry this stone around when your energies are depleted. Take some time to study this stone, see where your intuition takes you. Be like the child carefree and innocent. Your harvest will be plentiful if you let the energies of the sun nurture you and your aspirations. When a Sunstone appears in a reading, it is an indicator that things are are going well in the aspirant's life. Take the time to enjoy your life go out into the sun and find yourself a quiet place to contemplate your spiritual growth. It is okay to take a timeout, but be careful to not bask is the sun's rays for too long least you get burned. Contemplation on this stone will bring the sun's aspects into your life. It is important to remember that good times are very important, so celebrate the new day. Each day you wake up, breathing and alive is a chance to have a grad day. It is up to you to decided if today is a going to be a good day or not.

XX
Judgment
Pluto

Fire Opal

Here the aspirant has come to be judged. The people are floating in the abyss. The mountains loom in the background, but the aspirant does not look towards them; you only wish to be judged worthy of your deeds. They ask the Great Divine for forgiveness so they may be deemed worthy to cross the abyss. What you may fail to realize is that Judgment is always just and no matter what one thinks, they will never fool the Judge on judgment day. You are so committed and content that you did not realize that you were lost amongst the waves of the chasm. Like the Death card, Judgment its a warning; and it may feel like death, but the aspirant has made some bad choices and must now be judged. To be able to reach one's goals, you must live up to your Highest Ideals or they might become lost in the abyss of Judgment.

Fire Opal

Fire Opals are corresponded to the Judgment card. This stone represents justice and harmony. Fire Opal is a stone that is those who live a truthful life. Fire Opals are excellent stones to carry to alleviate emotional turmoil. The Fire Opal attracts negative energies so be careful when wearing one. Fire Opals come in a range of colors, from golden to dark red. They are also known for bringing the passion of fire to the aspirant's life. When Fire Opal comes up in a reading, it is an indicator that something is wrong and the situation is being judged. When Judgment starts to blow the horn, it is time to reevaluate the situation. It is not death, but life that awaits the aspirant. A Fire Opal may aid in the spiritual discipline of the aspirant. While contemplating this stone, keep in mind that it attracts as well as emits the energies one puts into it. So be careful what energies you project around this stone. Cleansing your stones regularly by utilizing one of the methods in this book will prevent misreading of the stones. One way to cleanse the energies from the stones is to let the sun hit it for a full day. It will be more beneficial to perform this task when the sun is bright with just a few clouds.

XXI
The World
Saturn

Pink Opal

The Lady holds two Wands; these Wands are reminiscent of the Magician and Chariot driver. The Great Four of the World are the Four Winds, Directions, Elements, etc. The wreath is a symbol of fertility. The aspirant has the whole world within reach, but must realize that to have everything is to have one's needs met in life and be content. This is an awesome achievement, but it is not the end of the quest; merely one achievement in a series of many. To obtain the World do not be greedy, you must be willing to give in order to get. You have been given a great opportunity to obtain worldly gifts, but keep in mind that to receive these gifts you must first show Perfect Love and Perfect Trust.

Pink Opal

Pink Opal has been corresponded to the World card. Carrying a Pink Opal will aid in the pursuits of Higher Spirituality by allowing the aspirant to comprehend that the material wealth is not needed to gain s spiritual well being. The Path is open, the World is at your feet, and all the elements are in place for the Goddess to guide you along the Path. When a Pink Opal appears in a reading, it is sign that things are going well for the aspirant. Opal brings the practitioner mental clarity, in divination, and studying purposes. Because, Opals tend to attract negative as well as positive energies, this stone should be cleansed on a regular basis. If one does not know how to cleanse their stones, look in the chapter at the beginning of this book. When a Pink Opal appears in one's life it is alerting the aspirant to the fact that the negative energies will take advantage of you. The World is in your hands do not let it go to your head.

Chapter Five: The Major Arcana

Chapter Six: The Minor Arcana
Swords - Air

I - Ace of Swords

Ace of Swords
Sodalite
The Divine is holding forth a sword crowned with an olive branch and fern. There are mountains visible on the horizon. The aspirant needs to take hold of the sword offered by the Divine. This tool will lead you on the journey to find Divine Inspiration. The sword represents Air, and you move your voice with the air, thus swords often represent words. The aspirant will need to wield the sword with love and care, because the sword cuts both ways, and when one does not watch what they are doing or saying things tend to come back on them. When the aspirant is offered the sword by the Divine hand one may only take it with pure intentions least you find yourself on the wrong Path. The Path to the mountains takes great endurance to achieve the summit. There may be many heartaches and crowning achievements, but perseverance brings you closer to the Divine

Sodalite
Attributed to the Ace of Swords is Sodalite. This stone brings joy and stability to the aspirant as you continue along the journey. However, watch what is being said least it come back to haunt you later on down the road. It has been said that words cut like a sword; fast and deep. Sodalite brings new beginnings and change to the aspirant's life. It also brings balance and inner peace. The Divine is reaching down to give you one of the tools needed on the journey. One should take up this tool and utilize it

to reach to heights. Try meditating with this stone, it may help in times of unbalance and bring you closer to the Divine. When meditating on this stone let the swords of white clouds take you ever deeper into the stone's inner most depth's. Try to imagine yourself within the stone, and let the stone's energies engulf you and take all the unwanted stress out of you. Let the stone's energies soothe away all your troubles,

II - Two of Swords

Two of Swords
White Agate

The aspirant sits in a contemplative state with a blindfold around your eyes. You hold aloft twin swords with your arms crossed. The abyss is behind you with small mountains looming on the horizon. The aspirant does not appear ready to traverse the abyss to reach the mountains of spirituality. Instead, you sit in meditation, preparing for the Initiation into spirituality. This is necessary to make such a journey. The aspirant is seated upon a stone bench with her back to the water. If you were to lose balance, you might fall backwards into the abyss and be lost in the waves of emotions. The aspirant must learn the lessons this card teaches. The lessons of this card are that it takes perseverance to achieve the heights of spirituality, but the rewards are all the sweeter. It Is better to go into Initiation with strength of will, rather then going in unprepared.

White Agate

The White Agate has been chosen to represent the Two of Swords. The White Agate brings peace, tranquility, and purity of the heart. When studying this stone, keep in mind that to utilize the energies of the White Agate you should center your mental forces through meditation. When a White Agate appears in a reading it shows the aspirant that there are trials ahead and they might be laborious, but the rewards will be fantastic. Spiritual development and balance are what is needed at this time. You must have Perfect Love and Perfect Trust to achieve purity of heart. This is a test of physical and mental skills. If you are at peace with yourself and others then the Path of wisdom will be revealed. If you are filled with corruption and hatred in your heart the Divine will know.

III - Three of Swords

Three of Swords
Red Agate

The Three of Swords is a card of sadness and sorrow. The aspirant's emotions are raining down on them. You must be prepared for the up-coming turmoil, because the storm is coming. If you do not seek the spiritual side of the situation you may feel lost in the deluge. Heartbreak or loss of love could be seen here, as depicted by the pierced heart. Times are not good for maters of the heart at this juncture, losses have occurred and now it is hard to be without that love. It may seem that going on is pointless, but you must. This time of trial will pass and the glow of the Hermit's lantern will soon reappear. Fret naught - the rain will dissipate soon, the sun will shine again, and the aspirant will find that happiness has returned. You must not give up hope. You need to pull out the swords so that the wounds may heal properly. The healing begins here with this realization; to start the healing process one must let go of what one loves to get through the heartache a whole lot faster than if you hold on to it forever. If you have lost someone and the pain seems too unbearable, try letting the Divine help you through this time of trouble. Pull out the swords and let the healing commence.

Red Agate

Attributed to the Three of Swords is the Red Agate. This stone teaches one to count their blessings. The Three of Swords is a card of loneliness and despair, but the Red Agate is the perfect stone for countering the effects of this depressing card. When this stone is drawn, it is a sign that something is lost. Do not dwell on it, however, there is a silver-lining to the rain-cloud. Meditating on this stone will increase one's ability to cope with the heartache and depression. Take this stone with you and keep it close so that its energies are readily available to you. Try to remember that things always get better with time and the energies of the Red Agate will help in the mending from the pain inflicted at this time. First things first; pull the swords out of the heart so the healing may start, and then give yourself the chance to fight off the melancholy. Go out to do something fun, let yourself have a little excitement; do not let the heartache take hold of you. When this stone comes up in a layout, try to recall any good times you have had in the past. This may be hard, but things will inevitably get better.

IV - Four of Swords

Four of Swords
Citrine

The aspirant is in a meditative state, with one sword as your foundation, and the remaining three pointing at the Chakras; the third eye, heart, and the solar plexus. The aspirant holds his hands in a steeple or praying position, with a blank look on your face as if in repose. A stained glass window that of a church bathes the aspirant in light. You have come here to meditate on what you have learned thus far. You have moved along the Path and you realize that you need to rest for a little while so there will be strength enough left to move forward. The aspirant has journeyed far and worked hard, you deserve a rest. Rest is good for the body, mind, and spirit; it is something everyone needs every once and a while. To sit back and contemplate the journey you have been on, and spend some time in meditation will enable you to regain a foot-hold in the mountain's steep slope.

Citrine

Citrine has been attributed to the Four of Swords. Citrine carries energies of healing inspiration and self-improvement. Meditating on this stone is a great way to connect to the latent energies of Citrine. It may just be what you need at this point in the journey. Citrine is believed to heal the spiritual self, lift the spirits, and add confidence to those with low self-esteem. Carrying this stone may help maintain a healthy outlook on life (such as eating healthy, exercising, etc.). When Citrine appears in a reading, it could be that you need to return to the spiritual by means of meditation and contemplation. Do not let this chance elude you, instead, seize the moment and make this time special. Utilize Citrine's energies to regain equilibrium and a renewed sense of self-worth. When all else fails, return to the basics. The healing Will commence once the aspirant realizes that you need the spiritual side of healing as well as the physical. Let the Divine guide you to the better things in life: Peace, Love, and Happiness.

V - Five of Swords

Five of Swords
Fossil Agate

The aspirant stands arrogantly over those you have bested. You do not see the mountains, but instead, you watch with joy at the anguish you have caused. The ego has taken over, you have won the day, but you have not achieved the heights of wisdom. Taking things by force does not accomplish the goals of the seeker, it only causes pain and suffering. Do not follow the same mistake; instead learn from it. Be mindful and have strength of character, so you may prevail over the situation. Remember that even when you win a battle, there is always someone out there bigger and better then you. You can not always win, no matter how good you think you are, or how strong you are; so do not trip over your over-inflated ego.

Fossil Agate

The Fossil Agate has been attributed to the Five of Swords. This Agate brings with it the ability to overcome obstacles, alleviate a stressful situation, and become more steadfast. When this stone appears in a reading, it is an indicator that there is a trial ahead; but with the right tools, skills, and attitude the outcome will be favorable. Do not rush into anything too quickly, be wise, and let the right time be on your side. The true test comes when one least expects it, so be prepared and you will come out ahead of the rest

VI - Six of Swords

Six of Swords
Yellow Turquoise

A man is rowing the boat along the water and a woman wrapped in her cloak sits next to a child. Is the man guiding the the boat over the abyss the aspirant, or is he guiding the aspirant? Either way the aspirant is on a trip. This card generally stands for travel of some sort. The two pillars are seen here in the two swords standing aside from the other four. The travelers seem to be heading across the abyss to the mountains beyond the shore; the trees attest to the harshness of the land. The water is choppy and the road is unsteady. Success may take some time, but it is always attainable with perseverance. The aspirant, whether being led or leading the way, is on a quest to find grander achievements. To gain a solid understanding, the aspirant must study this card and take the first steps to make it happen. Do not stop for anything along the way, you might become distracted and not make it to the final destination.

Yellow Turquoise

Yellow Turquoise has been associated to the Six of Swords. Turquoise assists in the matters of love, prosperity, good fortune, promotion of a friendship, and protection; there are excellent values to have when journeying into the unknown. Yellow Turquoise lends energies to the aspirant when you are traveling. When this stone shows up in a layout, it may be telling the aspirant to prepare for a journey soon. It could be a long awaited vacation, or a spiritual journey that awaits the aspirant. One may be moving to a new house, or location, or perhaps the aspirant is planing a trek up the mountain. Whatever the reason, carrying this stone will help protect you during these times; keep your goal in mind so that you do not veer from your Path. The Yellow Turquoise is a fantastic stone to meditate upon. It will alleviate the pain of a lost friendship and help you move on with your life. The Yellow Turquoise may also protect the possessor from others wanting to do harm. Keep safe on the road to success, but remember that you will never know what is on the other side of the tracks unless you go and look; to be adventurous, do not be afraid to go out into the world and see what you can find. Meditate on this stone to generate a sense of freedom. If you wish to achieve success you must take the initiative and move forward. Start today the world is full of wonder, and excitement.

VII - Seven of Swords

Seven of Swords
Indian Bloodstone

Here the aspirant is carrying away many swords leaving two swords behind you, standing side-by-side. These represent the two pillars. You have the swords by the blades, not the hilt, you must be extremely careful not to let them slip; that would be catastrophic. You seem to be sneaking off with the swords. Is the aspirant a thief in the night? Are you stealing goods or just joyous to have so much? The aspirant should be careful at this time, the swords, or words are sharp and when you wield your words unintentionally they cut deep. Whether you have stolen these items or won them in some game of chance does not matter, you must think of the words you speak, they are like double edged blades, they cut in both directions. It is always best to be straight forward, do not sneak around; an untrustworthy nature will lead to your downfall in the end. Watch what you say, be true to your word, and do not forget that we are only as good as our word.

Indian Bloodstone

The Indian Bloodstone is corresponded to the Seven of Swords. Folklore says that wearing a bloodstone would make the possessor invisible for the stone dazzles the eyes of all those who see it. This may be how the aspirant is escaping with all those swords. Carrying a bloodstone may also aid in the defense against others' deception. This stone gives courage to those who have to conquer a particularly difficult task and lends logic, protection, and wisdom to those who may be facing danger. When this stone makes an appearance in a layout, it may be pointing out that the aspirant needs some protection to keep them safe from negative forces. Meditating on an Indian Bloodstone will bring on dreams of the future. By placing a Bloodstone under your pillow while sleeping, you may have divinatory dreams. Bloodstones have been said to be used by soldiers as a talisman to keep them safe during battle. When using an Indian Bloodstone on a regular basis, be sure to cleans it often to get rid of unwanted built up energies.

VIII - Eight of Swords

Eight of Swords
Unakite

The aspirant stands bound, isolated, and surrounded by eight swords. You stand in a puddle of water and the tide has shifted to the abyss. The aspirant has failed to make it to the heights, and now is stuck with obstacles surrounding you. The aspirant may feel hopeless in your situation, but you can make it out of this mess and continue to move forward if you realize the lessons of the Eight of Swords card. You may feel bound but there is always a way out of even the toughest predicaments; there is wisdom in this learning. The aspirant only needs to relax and think their way through the circumstances and they will make it through unscathed. Use your words to your advantage and the ties will loosen and free you. This has only been a learning experience, so live and learn.

Unakite

The Unakite stone has been placed with the Eight of Swords. Unakite in a layout lets the aspirant be aware of the trial that ensues. To get through this time of trouble, think about the things that have been bothering you. Is your job unsatisfactory and will not let you move forward? Are you in a relationship full of arguments and lies? What ever the reason, it is best to know how you become stagnant in the first place. When meditating upon this stone, let your intuitive nature take over, it may help to alleviate some of the stress. The virtues of this stone lend energies to attract a new relationship; whether friends or lovers, is up to the aspirant. When carrying this stone around, know that the Unakite fills one with happiness and joy. This stone lends help when finding and utilizing the concepts of Perfect Love and Perfect Trust, or unconditional love.

IX - Nine of Swords

Nine of Swords
Green Fluorite

The aspirant has awakened from a bad dream. The swords (words) have come back to haunt you and now you sit upon the bed with your head cradled in your hands; trying not to see what is before you. The aspirant must take action to right the wrong that has caused this troubling dream. The aspirant needs to realize that you have made these nightmares manifest, and you are the only one who can tame these troubling dreams. One can tweak things to change the future outcome. To right what is wrong you should learn that to fix the situation to rectify whatever it is you have done. Whether it was cursing at someone or telling a lie, the Nine of Swords teaches that when you use people for personal gain, it eventually comes back to haunt the aspirant; do not think for a moment that your words will not come back to disturb the flow of energy. Whether meant for ill or not does not matter the wave of energy is still set in motion. It will be written in the karmic records, and it is up to you to deal with them.

Green Fluorite

Green Fluorite has been associated with he Nine of Swords. Fluorite is soothing and offers protection to the one who bears it. When Green Fluorite shows up in a reading, it is to let you know that something is hiding deep within, the aspirant's dreams or psyche. Green Fluorite is great for those working in the astral plain. When this stone is used in meditation it helps the aspirant to release tensions even ones that may be unknown to you. Green Fluorite can clear one's consciousness of unwanted turmoil. Carrying one of these stones around with you will protect you against psychic attacks and other negative energies. A student may wish to meditate upon this stone before commencing their studies, as the stone's energies will open the doors of knowledge. It also clears the mind of unwanted or unnecessary clutter, and opens the thought process. Meditation with this stone will increase one's spiritual wisdom. When Green Fluorite appears in a layout, try to remember the Hermetic Principle: "As Above, So Below;" this is the inspiration of the seeker of the Mysteries. When one is lost in the abyss, this can be a reminder that the Great divine is with you always.

X - Ten of Swords

Ten of Swords
Black Agate

The aspirant is motionless, pinned to the ground. Blood flows forth from your wounds; the swords have come back to put an end to ego. This is a grim card, the darkened clouds of the storm are lifting though and the light is shining once again. The mountains are visible and the aspirant looks towards the horizon. You must get up and head to the heights of spirituality. The aspirant has been hurt by your words, whether they were of your own or from another is only known by the aspirant. You may feel helpless to get out of this predicament, but you can, all you have too do is pull out the swords, and let the healing commence. Do not let this ordeal be the end; it is only as bad as you let it be. The aspirant must learn from the mistakes of the past. This card speaks of one who has been dishonest, untrustworthy, or has broken their oath; although, you might make amends by keeping your word, you cannot seem to get over this time of despair. Keep in mind that there is light on the horizon. Do not despair, this is not the end of the journey, you must not allow yourself to let this opportunity slip past you.

Black Agate

The Black Agate is associated with the Ten of Swords. The Black Agate has the energies to dispel the negativity of the Ten of Swords. When a Black Agate appears in in a reading, it is signaling to the aspirant that something is wrong in your life. Try meditating on this stone and you might be amazed at how much better you will feel afterwards. Studying with a Black Agate nearby may help to discover how you got in such a predicament. The Black Agate has the qualities of other black stones such as banishing negative energies, so carry this stone with you to detour unwanted forces.

Page of Swords

Page of Swords
Yellow Agate

The aspirant stands on a hill top looking out over the land, but there are higher mountains in the background. The aspirant holds the sword aloft, but you are not in battle at this time. There are birds circling in the air overhead. The aspirant has a message on the way. The Page is a messenger, and this Page has information to convey to you so pay heed. You must not stop here, this is but a tiny hill; a small accomplishment. The aspirant has manifested into the Page perhaps you have an important message to deliver. You have gained a foot hold on the mountain, but the true test comes later when you climb the heights of the mountains summit. This is a lesser accomplishment then that of what you hunger for, but it is an achievement none the less. Learn the lessons this card had to teach so you may move forward on the Path. Although, you may have reached a goal by making it to this point, there is so much more awaiting you. Keep on the road to enlightenment. Do not stop now that you have accomplished so little, there is so much more to come. The Page brings a message to you; when on the Path watch for pitfalls, they are every where. Keep ever vigilant so you do not fall prey to the people who are not looking out for your best interest. When you do reach the heights you so desire, and you will one day, keep in mind that there are always some adventures to go on. The road does not stop, it continues ever forward even after death. Do not let your dreams slip away, chase them down, and when you do catch them do not let them go.

Yellow Agate

Corresponded to the Page of Swords is the Yellow Agate. Agates are great stones to improve conversational skills; a good characteristic for the Page, who brings messages to the aspirant. The Yellow Agate lends its energies to the aspirant so you may receive the message and learn from it. When a Yellow Agate appears in a spread, it brings with it a message for the aspirant to look deeper into the Mysteries. When meditating on this stone, remember to utilize the stone's attributes, such as; courage, strength, and valor. This stone will help you overcome any mishaps. This is a good stone to carry when finding out what the Universe is trying to tell you.

Knight of Swords

Knight of Swords
Turquoise

The aspirant is charging into action as fast as the stead will take you. You are prepared for battle, and are covered with armor to protect your soft skin from the trials to come. With your sword held aloft and at the ready you are prepared to do battle; but who or what are you waring with? There is a majestic butterfly on the horse, this may represent air. To reach the hight of spirituality, one must live a spiritual life; what is needed now is meditation and contemplation. When one's life is out of sync, they should get back in touch with the spiritual side. The aspirant would be wise to stop and think before charging into battle you might not like what you encounter. The Knight is brave and valiant, but only a fool would not pay heed to the dangers ahead.

Turquoise

Turquoise has been assigned to the Knight of Swords. Like

the Knight, the Turquoise offers protection to the aspirant. When worn, Turquoise lends its abilities to alleviate stress when you may not be able to handle things yourself. You may need a little help from others to get you through these troubling times. When this stone shows up in a reading, it is advising the aspirant that the time has come to meditate upon the Turquoise stone to regain equilibrium in your life. When you are in need of help the Knight will charge in to protect you. If a Turquoise stone shows up in a spread it is telling the aspirant that you are going at things too fast. Slow down and think things through, life doesn't have to be so fast. Take the time to enjoy your life every once and a while. When meditating on this stone remember that when you wield your words haphazardly things tend to get thrown out of whack.

Queen of Swords

Queen of Swords
Golden Jade

The Queen looks out with determination on her face, and she wields a rather large sword. There are no mountains visible only a small creek and some dead trees. The land looks bleak and stark. This Queen wields a huge burden, but there is a softer side depicted in the butterflies and the cherubs on the throne, which balance the spiritual and the mundane. The crescent moons on the throne represent the Goddess' will presented in this card. The aspirant may not be happy to perform the duties that are set before you, but even those in such a high stations must do the work necessary to get the job done. The work of the Divine should come first. Try to relax, and do not take things to the extreme; life is too short for that.

Golden Jade

Golden Jade has been attributed to the Queen of Swords. Jade lends its energies to bring peace and serenity into the aspirant's life. When a Jade appears in a spread, it is alerting the aspirant that good luck is on your side and a tranquil life can be obtained through diligence of character. Golden Jade brings one nearer to wisdom, comforts one's fears and keeps a peaceful mind. Golden Jade is also know to repel harmful emotions and magick. Meditation with this stone during times of trouble will help even the odds and promote peace, love, and joy.

King of Swords

King of Swords
Lemon Chrysoprase

This King is stern faced like his Queen counter-part. He holds his sword at the ready, but he is not wearing any battle armor at this time. The throne is quite small compared to the other suits; only visible with its butterflies and cherubs. There is a single butterfly between a waxing and a waning moon. There are birds flying above the throne, a sure sign of a message coming soon. The King is always ready to fight. To defend the kingdom and his people, he must keep his domain safe; and through him, all law is kept. This can be a tough way to live. He must not be rash or else those around him will fail to see his wisdom and authority, and he might be over-thrown. To stay seated upon the throne, you cannot throw your weight around to gain notoriety; it is only through a civil tongue that the King gets his work done. The aspirant has to understand that to be in such a high stature you must be willing to fight for what is right; but also know when to be at peace. The aspirant would be wise to learn from this King, he has much to teach.

Lemon Chrysoprase

The Lemon Chrysoprase has been corresponded with the King of Swords. Lemon Chrysoprase brings grounding, healing, good fortune, self-expression, and keeps the internal energy strong to promote a well-balanced constitution. This stone has a calming affect and brings a connection to royalty. Being a court stone, the Chrysoprase allows you to integrate the mental with the physical by showing you that your body is a temple, and your mind is of the Divine Spirit. Chrysoprase brings the aspirant diligence in contemplating a long term goal. When trying to achieve the greatness of the King, remember to stay humble. This stone Lends its energies to improve vision, memory, and speech; faculties that are necessary for any King to remain the King. This stone helps to alleviate emotional disturbances, and promotes emotional healing.

Chapter Seven: The Minor Arcana
Wands - Fire

I - Ace of Wands

Ace of Wands
Spinel

The aspirant is being offered another tool from the Great Divine whose hand appears out of the clouds. There is a home on top of a hill with a river that separates the aspirant from the hill. To forge the river, the aspirant needs to take what is being offered from the Divine hand to Cross the abyss and obtain what is on the other side. When the aspirant learns the lessons of this card, they will be satisfied with what you have achieved; but you should never stop learning. Keep in mind that you must make steady progress along the Path so you do not become lost in the maze of life. Take what is being offered and use it to attain the heights. You have what it takes to reach the destination you so desire. The Divine will not wait forever, so pick up the tool and use it to find your way along the Path.

Red Spinel

The Red Spinel is attributed to the Ace of Wands card. Red Spinel in a layout brings the power of change. The Ace of Wands is held aloft by the Great Unknown. The aspirant must take hold of the staff, and use it to scale the mountain's heights to achieve spiritual enlightenment. Red Spinel lends energies and power to make one aware of your inner creativity and personal power. You may become aware of your potential in a creative sense. Spinel will bring balance and new experiences to one's life. When a Red Spinel shows up in a reading it is a herald to the aspirant to get moving along the Path, and use your staff to keep balanced.

II - Two of Wands

Two of Wands
Tigereye

Here the aspirant is contemplating a globe. The two pillars are represented here once again. The twin Wands stand as the two pillars One of the Wands is attached to the wall, secure, but at the ready. The other Wand is in the aspirant's hand. You are ready for the trip, the journey up the mountain. Is there a companion who has not showed up yet? The aspirant is once again the Middle Pillar. You must go forth to the far reaches of the globe so you can learn the lessons of this card. The aspirant has a long journey ahead of you, even if you are alone in this trek there will be help along the way. The staff will aid you in remaining balanced when the Path becomes rough. You have what it takes to make it all he way to the top.

Tigereye

Associated to the Two of Wands, is the Tigereye stone. Within this stone the polarities are found; the good and the bad, the the dark and light, the male and the female. The aspirant is in deep contemplation with this stone. The Tigereye is a fantastic stone to meditate on. When meditating on this stone let its shimmering golden bands take you deep into your meditation. You may wish to meditate on the future. The Tigereye is a lucky stone carrying one will bring this energy to you. To move along the Path, you should be careful to stay away from the entanglements that are inevitably in the road to higher understanding. Contemplation of the past, present, and the future will prepare you to face the many obstacles along the way. The Path is rough at times, but keep a hold of your wand and perseverance will bring the aspirant through these times.

III - Three of Wands

Three of Wands
Red Jasper

Here the aspirant stands atop a small rise looking over the abyss to the mountains. You see the boats that will cross that expanse, and know the time to get moving is near. The aspirant is now standing closer to the destination, ready to forge ahead to the heights. The aspirant is eager to get started. With your staff in hand, the tool given to you by the Great Unknown, you will reach those heights if you do not let anything get in your way. However, you must keep in mind that this will not be an easy trek; but a rather difficult one. It will be full of adventure and fun at times and disappointment and sorrow at others. Do not give up at the first sign of trouble; even though it may seem easier to throw away the staff and say "I quit;" it is the wise aspirant who stays on course and does not stop for anything. Those are the ones who get the greatest rewards in the end.

Red Jasper

The Red Jasper has been assigned to the Three of Wands. Red Jasper is an exceptional stone for healing emotions, and promote inner balance. This stone brings the traveler protection on a dark night. Even though the aspirant is traveling the Path of light, there may be a time when you are walking in the dark, this stone will illuminate the Path so that you can find your way. This stone will help to battle the malignant forces that may be trying to divert the traveler from your course. When troubled by nightmares try sleeping with a Red Jasper under your pillow; it will lend energies to alleviate and subdue the troublesome dreams. Red Jasper is excellent for opening the heart chakra. When you go on a dream quest, you traverse the boundaries of time and space into the realms of dreams, extending over the far reaches of the imagination. Red Jasper strengthens the inner self against any psychic attack, so be sure to carry this stone in a bag or pocket to utilize the energies when traveling.

IV - Four of Wands

Four of Wands
Rhyolite

The two people central in this card are holding their arms up in victory. They appear to be male and female. Are they coming together as lovers? Is this their ceremony uniting the two souls? Or is this a game of some sort and these two the winners? The aspirant is one of the two in this celebration, and whether you are uniting with another or winning a game, the aspirant is going through some good times. There are Paths to walk, and mountains to climb, but for now bask in the joy of The moment; chase your dreams. The four wands stand side-by-side making the two pillars of the polarities, with the aspirant as the Middle Pillar. The fruit and flowers are symbols of fertility and a plentiful harvest. A bridge spans the abyss and the aspirant can reach the mountains with ease. There is a great achievement happening at this juncture in the aspirant's life. Have your fun now, but do not terry too long the Hermit awaits. Do not stop thinking of the future, the journey has just begun.

Rhyolite

Rhyolite is assigned to the Four of Wands. Rhyolite is a lesser known gemstone, but it creates a more health outlook on life and helps brighten the physical health of the aspirant. Rhyolite can light the fires of creativity within the soul, so carry this stone around to boost your creativity. Meditate upon this stone to bring positive change and progress to one's spiritual growth. When the aspirant questions their ability to grow spiritually, this stone is a reminder that you are on the right Path. This stone calls for the union of two souls and sparks passion into a relationship. When Rhyolite comes up in a reading, it is an indicator that the aspirant's life is on track and it is time to celebrate. If the aspirant is united with another this stone may be a reminder to keep renewing your love.

V - Five of Wands

Five of Wands
Banded Agate

The aspirant appears to be in battle at this time, but it is only a game of the youth to hone one's skills? You hold up your hands in victory, you have won the day. While this depicts conflict and violence in the aspirant's life, victory over one's opponents is most likely to come. This card is alerting the aspirant to a conflict. When things are going wrong in a situation remember to be humble even if you are right. Sometimes you have to temper your ego to stay out of trouble. Sometimes the best victory is not having to fight in the first place. There are mountains in the background, but the aspirant does not look to them for guidance.

Do not dilly dally too long, the Path looms ahead and it is time to move forward.

Banded Agate

Banded Agate is associated to the Five of Wands. The Banded Agate brings the aspirant inner peace when conflicting with others. This stone has latent energies that bands together rivalries. When you find yourself at odds with someone, try meditating on this stone. Meditation will help to bring closure to the issue, or give you an idea of how to resolve it. To resolve the aggressive energies within yourself, and others around you, utilize this stone's energies. When a Banded Agate comes up in a spread it is a warning of a conflict that may ensue or has already been set in motion. To counter this Issue, contemplate a Banded Agate, use its energy of valor and strength to find a peaceful way out of the matter.

VI - Six of Wands

Six of Wands
Snowflake Obsidian

The aspirant sits upon a grey horse which is covered with cloth and you hold a wand with a wreath tied to the tip with a red ribbon. The rider also wears a wreath on his head. The aspirant seems to be looking off into the distance, perhaps you are contemplating a quest. There is no confrontation at this time. The aspirant is among friendly faces, luck is on your side, the goal has been achieved and everyone celebrates. Maybe you defeated a dragon and saved the city, whatever the accomplishment was, now is the time to celebrate. Let go of your inhibition and relax, life will commence after the party. Then when your back on the road of spirituality you will be tranquil and at peace.

Snowflake Obsidian

Snowflake Obsidian is corresponded with the Six of Wands. This stone brings inner balance and equilibrium to one's life. Snowflake Obsidian restores your outlook and demeanor to be healthier than it was before. This stone promotes spiritual growth through meditation. When this stone appears in a reading it is allowing the aspirant to stay balanced. While meditating on the Snowflake Obsidian do not forget to envision a peaceful and tranquil, existence in Perfect Balance with the Universe. This stone has the ability to absorb energy from the immediate surroundings, this could be a good thing if you are nervous or having an anxiety attack. With this stone you can channel energies to or away from yourself, or your Sacred Space. The Snow flake Obsidian may be used to clear the mind, but it can be a tricky stone to work with, so be sure to cleanse it regularly. When this stone shows up in a layout it is telling the aspirant that your life is balanced and going good. You can relax now that you have attained this goal.

VII - Seven of Wands

Seven of Wands
Amber

This card reminds one of the old game: "The King of the mountain," where the rest of the group tries to push there way on top of the mountain, to gain the top position, only to be attacked themselves. Unseen attackers threaten to push the aspirant down from the position you have attained to the abyss below. You must be ready to battle the unknown, but you seem worried about something in this time of unrest. The battle has come, and you must stand and fight. There is a time for peace, and then there is the time to fight for what you believe in. The aspirant must realize that to be on top is a huge responsibility. When you reach the summit, you have gained much, but there are always more Paths to tread; keep on moving along your Path. The aspirant feels Under attack right now, but you can win this fight and move forward.

Amber

Attributed to the Seven of Wands is Amber. This stone has qualities of a soothing nature. When conflict arrises, whether it is a mental or mortal adversary, Amber is an ideal stone for restoring balance to the energy emanating from the brain. Amber promotes balance in mental and physical health, and lends its energies to bring success into one's life. When an Amber appears in a reading it is to alert the aspirant to inert energies that may cause conflict. Meditation on this stone can help restore energy and strengthens your commitment, and your will to move forward toward success. However, you must put forth the effort to attain a fulfilled life. When you are feeling down, Amber can lend energies to alleviate the melancholy.

VIII - Eight of Wands

Eight of Wands
Brecciated Jasper

The eight wands seem poised for attack. There are no mountains in sight, only a house on top of a small hill. The aspirant may find things are weighing down on you. A change may be in order at this time. The Eight of Wands is an indication of transformation, the rearranging of one's mundane life is necessary at this point in the journey. A spiritual or astral change may also be needed. The Eight of Wands shows that others are involved in a attack. You may feel pressured by an unseen force at the moment but know that the Divine watches over you. The aspirant would be wise to revert to the Ace to find refuge. The way to find the Path again is to pick yourself up, dust yourself off, and get back on track. This is only a temporary set back, do not let it get to you head. The Eight of Wands shows that others are involved. The aspirant would be wise to accept change to move beyond this situation. It may seem that events are moving too fast, you may feel like grasping for the wands, but that would be futile at this point. What is important right now is to remain focused on your journey.

Brecciated Jasper

Brecciated Jasper is corresponded to the Eight of Wands. Brecciated Jasper has strong energies of protection and can be used when under attack from an unseen enemy. This stone is highly useful when dealing with stressful situations, and is used for divination and or a vision quest. Those who suffer from a bipolar disorder, manic-depression, or even Schizophrenia, can benefit from this stone; as it is known to calm the mind and balance to body and soul. The red of a Brecciated Jasper helps to improve one's overall physical energy and vitality, this is useful in this time of unrest where strength and endurance is needed to sooth the nerves. When a brecciated Jasper comes up in a reading, it is telling the aspirant that some external force is trying to attack. To counter this aggression, meditate on this stone and carry it to strengthen your will. Things are not going as planned at this juncture, so try something new. Remember when you are feeling down and out, the Great Divine will lend a helping hand and the latent energies of this stone is an excellent source of Divine Inspiration.

IX - Nine of Wands

Nine of Wands
African Jade

The aspirant looks out suspiciously at your surroundings. you have been injured and seems to be waiting for another attack. There are hills visible in the background. You have been beat up, beat down, but not beat into submission; the aspirant still stands and will live to see another fight. The aspirant would be wise to learn from this encounter and move on. To be able to win the day or the battle, you need to gain knowledge so you can persevere. There will be many battles ahead, but the aspirant can rest easy for now; the fight has been won and the celebration awaits. If you wish to win in the future, take some time to hone your skills. Look to the mountains and your future, do not get caught up in the victory of the battles you have won, or you may experience bigger losses in the end.

African Jade

African Jade is associated to the Nine of Wands. This stone lends its energies to bring inner peace and balance to the aspirant. The African Jade has many healing qualities to help alleviate the pains of the battle, so do not hesitate to carry this stone with you so that the healing process can begin. Meditating upon this stone will allow one to receive wisdom and gain enlightenment to reveal negative emotions. When African Jade makes an appearance in a layout, it is to alert the aspirant to an upcoming event that may be already in full swing. Take caution in these times of turmoil.

X - Ten of Wands

Ten of Wands
Autumn Jasper

Here we have the aspirant straining under the weight of a heavy load of Wands. The Wands have leaves on them to symbolize life and fertility. The burden may seem to great, however, the desire to persevere is evident. The aspirant struggles at this time, but the final outcome is near. Even though you are not at the heights of the mountain top, the destination is not much further. Be sure not to over-embellish your work, or you might hurt yourself and you cannot work at all. If the aspirant is to learn anything from this card, it would be to take on only that what you can handle; do not over-exert or over-commit yourself to the point of possible injury. There are better ways; easier ways to obtain the same results. Take up the tool the Great Divine has offered you at the beginning of the suit, and use it to gain the heights of spirituality.

Autumn Jasper

Assigned to the Ten of Wands is the Autumn Jasper. This variation of Jasper is a good source of physical strength, an excellent attribute when one is carrying such a large load. When the aspirant is feeling weighed down with the burdens of life, this stone lends its energies to strengthen one's resolve. Carrying Autumn Jasper can put the aspirant in charge of the situation. When this stone appears in a reading, it may be telling you to not take on too many burdens. When it feels like you are over-tasked the trick is to take one small step at a time. Meditation on this stone will bring insight on how to get through troubled times to reach one's destination

XI - Page of Wands

Page of Wands
Wood Agate

The aspirant stands in the desert with sand dunes all around. You stand motionless and you are contemplating the leaves of the Wand. The flames seen coming out of your hat and boots may symbolize the flame of desire. As you stand idly by, your faith blows away with the wind. Clenching at your dreams is as futile as trying to grip the sand. Idleness is okay for a moment, but if you wish to gain greater learning you must embrace greater understanding. The Page is a messenger so watch for news coming your way. The wise aspirant will know that the Page comes with good news. The wand which was offered in the Ace of this suit is used to navigate the treacherous terrain so one can make it to the destination safely.

Wood Agate

The Wood Agate stone is corresponded to the Page of Wands. This is an excellent stone for diplomats, as it improves their conversational skills. When carried, this stone lends its energies to improve one's tact and social behavior. While meditating on this stone, keep in mind what it is you wish to accomplish, but remember that in order to achieve your dreams you need to stay grounded in the real world as well. When a Wood Agate appears a reading, it may be a message that you are day-dreaming and not pressing forward in your pursuit of a peaceful life. Use the energy of this stone to ground or help you find the Path once again.

XII - Knight of Wands

Knight of Wands
Mahogany Obsidian

The aspirant in seen here clad in armor, holding a Wand. The steed rears into action. The flames on your helmet symbolize the fires of your desire. The salamander on your chest represents honor. This Knight is ready for action, with a burning desire to move forward towards the pyramids that beckon you to great rewards. Like the sands in an hourglass, the aspirant moves on, draining yourself of all substance. The desire is great and the need for action is strong. You go into battle willingly, with lust in your heart. The aspirant must keep in mind that the sandy mountains may not be there long enough to climb; the sand shifts in the wind. Once to aspirant learns these things, you can set your goals for the Ideals of a higher plane.

Mahogany Obsidian

Mahogany Obsidian is attributed to the Knight of Wands. When carrying a Mahogany Obsidian, remember to cleanse it regularly, because it will attract energies from all directions. Since Mahogany Obsidian if formed by molten lava, it is ideal for spiritual walks into the abyss of mental understanding. This stone is excellent for creating a protective shield around you while you slumber. It is known to protect one's dreams. When a Mahogany Obsidian appears in a reading, it is spurring the aspirant into action. The horse is ready and the Knight beckons the aspirant to continue along the Path. When meditating on this stone, be sure your energies are well intended or the negative energies you put into the stone will reflect back o

XIII - Queen of Wands

Queen of Wands
Red Aventurine

The Queen sits upon a big decorative throne with its sunflowers and beast. The aspirant is seen here holding a sunflower in one hand and a Wand in the other. The aspirant's faithful feline sits at your feet standing guard, while the cunning fox holds the robes around your neck. There are sand dunes standing behind you, but you do not seek them out. The aspirant is seen here as the Queen who is in control of things; there is no joy in her face as she looks off into the distance without a smile. The aspirant would be wise to learn the lessons this Queen has to offer. The sand mountains are illusive and difficult to obtain they may never be scaled, and the aspirant has to go in search of a more solid ground to climb. To obtain the mountain of substance, you must achieve the spiritual understanding of the Hermit.

Red Aventurine

Red Aventurine has been assigned to the Queen of Wands. This stone brings peace, well being, and strengthens the heart. Red Aventurine enhances creativity so you can endure the rigors of everyday life, and enhances creativity. Use Aventurine to find direction in life or use it to balance the course of one's life. Corresponded to Mars, Red Aventurine has a fiery quality to it. This Queen has the passion to continue along the Path so when Red Aventurine appears in a layout, it is telling the aspirant that the time has come to use your creative abilities and passion to press forward. Carrying this stone helps to raise one's inner strength and overall energy. Meditation on this stone can bring healing on an emotional level, so try holding it when you feel down or looney. Meditation can help reveal the inner forces affecting one's life.

XIV - King of Wands

King of Wands
Red Malachite

This King does not wear the armor of battle, only stately robes, his crown and the cuffs of his sleeves bear flames on them, a sign of the heat of passion or the flame of desire. Salamander graces the dais, the King's throne, and robes. The salamanders have their tails in their mouths as a sign of infinity or the oroboros. The King appears serious, and seems ready to jump up and spring into action. The King holds his wand at the ready and clenches his fist tight. Although, at peace at the moment the aspirant is full of burning passion at this time. The aspirant is on edge and is ready to fight . One must keep in mind that to be King you must be prepared to defend the realm and the people. Continue to move along the Path to the greater things that await the wise aspirant. You are at peace, and your desire to battle does not serve you well. The Salamanders show the aspirant the fiery side of one's emotions, do not allow the emotional state to take hold of you, it is not congruent at this juncture of the journey.

Red Malachite

With the King of Wands comes Red Malachite, malachite brings inner strength, loyalty, and is a very soothing stone. When a Red Malachite shows up in a reading, it is indicating that you may not be in touch with your feelings. Meditation upon this stone will help you discover how you feel about certain situations. Meditation upon this stone will bring visions of the future and tell you when you must take up the role of leadership. Carrying this stone enhances one's abilities to perform and carry out business deals. Since the King of Wands is a business man, he must be diplomatic in his dealings; Red Malachite lends its energies to this cause. You may want to utilize this stone to get in touch with the Ancient Ones, they can aid in the Divination of the future.

Chapter Eight: Minor Arcana
Cups: Water

I - Ace of Cups

Ace of Cups
Red Coral

Here the aspirant is being offered one more tool from the Great Divine. The aspirant must be ready and willing to embrace the emotional aspect of the journey to be able to achieve what you have set off to do. The dove dips the holy bread into the Chalice and from the Chalice blessings flow forth. The aspirant is being given the holy Chalice of emotions. This is an opportunity to free yourself of emotional baggage you may have accumulated in the past. Everyone has emotions, they are a part of life, but when you learn to control them, you are all the better for it; but at the same time don't keep your emotions locked up so no one can see them. When you are in control of your emotions, you can continue to move along the Path. The aspirant would be wise to learn the lessons of this card, take the Chalice and journey to the Heights. One who seeks to be all they can is one who has all they need. If the aspirant feels lost in the other cards in this suit, he can review the Ace to learn what is being taught to them by the Universe.

Red Coral

Red Coral is attributed to the Ace of Cups. The lore encompassing the remedial values of Coral is as diverse as the astrological correspondences. Coral has the ability to boost one's ego and help maintain a balance of emotion so they can come back to the beginning of the Suit. Once again, the aspirant is being offered emotional health from the grace of the Great Divinity, therefore, take hold of what is being offered. According to old folklore, Coral was said to lose its color when the wearer became ill, but was believed to return when the bearer became healthy again. The Coral stone should be contemplated to restore one's emotional health, outlook, and balance. If burdens from other stone's energies are upon the aspirant, she can use the energy of Coral as a starting point to restore emotional stability and mental health.

II - Two of Cups

Two of Cups
Red Garnet

The sign of health between the man and woman speaks of fertility, love, and happiness. The polarities have come together in the aspirant's life in order to bring greater rewards. Here the man has a wreath of flowers around his head as a symbol of fertility. The woman in turn also has a wreath of the leaves, representing the masculine side of the feminine. The aspirant has brought both into his or her life and this perfect balance will bring great rewards with it. The aspirant is now finding love, perhaps not a lover, but a love of some sort none the less. There are no mountains visible, only a small hill. It is a time to work together with the one you love to achieve your spiritual growth.

Red Garnet

The Red Garnet is assigned to the Three of Cups. When dealing with emotional and psychological issues, it is wise to carry this stone to help restore self-esteem. One can also utilize a Red Garnet to promote a clear, retentive mind. When meditating upon this stone, remember that friendship is especially important in life. Friends lift your spirits and hold you up in times of need. When this stone appears in a layout, it is reminding you to call upon friendship to unite one another. This stone has the ability to attract another to you, or sexuality in relationships. Red Garnet is said to protect the possessor from from unwanted energies of others – whether asleep or awake. It can help protect against nightmares or depression.

III - Three of Cups

Three of Cups
Rose Quartz

Three Goddesses are seen holding their Chalices high in a salute. Times are good, the fertility of the land is great, and the harvest is near. Things are going well, but do not overindulge in the finery of life; remember to look to the future as well. If the aspirant does not wish to lose what they have, they must be wise and learn from this card. The one who takes for granted the gifts the Goddess provides you is the one who loses everything to greed.

Rose Quartz

To the Three of Cups the Rose Quartz is joined to combine the energy of the two. When meditation is performed with this stone, place it on the heart chakra to promote healing of emotional sorrows, pains, and wounds. Carrying a Rose Quartz will help increase one's compassion and develop the ability to forgive those who have emotional damage. When this stone comes up in a layout, it is admonishing the aspirant to move forward in life. Carrying this stone will help one to do this comfortably and alleviate the negative energies working against them. This stone can also be called upon when you are feeling lonely and will improve harmony in relationships as well. The Goddess is ever present in this stone, so carry it with you when you find that you are in need of her touch.

IV - Four of Cups

Four of Cups
Sugilite

The aspirant sits in meditative repose atop a hill, leaning against a tree. The hand that reaches forth is to offer the Fourth Cup. The aspirant does not take notice of this gift as she contemplates being the tree, not realizing that the Divine is offering her a greater gift. Three other Cups sit empty, devoid of substance. In the distance rises the mountains, the true destination the aspirant longs for. The aspirant must learn to not only be content with what you have, but to strive ever forward.

Sugilite

Sugilite is connected with the Four of Cups. When a Sugilite appears in a layout, it is telling the aspirant they are not paying attention to what the Divine is offering them. Use your intuition at these times, it is very important. If the aspirant wishes to meditate upon this stone, they need to be ever mindful of their intuition; let your gut feeling guide you along the Path of enlightenment. Carrying a Sugilite can affect one's outlook and boost the intuitive nature of the aspirant. The divine is offering the aspirant many gifts, don't let them slip away.

V - Five of Cups

Five of Cups
Blue Chalcedony

The aspirant sits contemplating two Cups that have broken with the contents spilled out. He does not look upon the two remaining Cups that are still intact, but instead dwells on what is lost. There is a bridge across the river, but he does not, or cannot, cross the abyss at this time; he chooses to stay here with his losses. The aspirant must pull himself together, though the loss is great. One needs to gather up what is left, and continue along the journey. This can be a hard thing to do when one is so distraught and the emotions are in turmoil. One must remember that what is lost is lost – so take up the remaining Chalices and move forward. Sometimes we get what we want, sometimes we get what we need, and then there are times we get what we deserve. Don't spend too much time dwelling on the mistakes of life, instead learn from this error to ensure that it does not happen again and keep your feet on the Path.

Blue Chalcedony

Blue chalcedony has been attributed to the Five of Cups. With this stone, the aspirant can heighten the mind to alleviate mental disorders. The Blue Chalcedony helps to steady the thoughts from dwelling on the negative aspects of the situation. The Blue Chalcedony has the ability to relive nightmares and fear of the unknown. It also lends its energies to help alleviate the pain of depression and promotes self-esteem and courage. When a Blue Chalcedony comes up in a reading, it is telling the aspirant that there are brighter days to come – so don't fret.

VI - Six of Cups

Six of Cups
Blue Lace Agate

The younger girl offers the older person a gift of fertile emotions. All of the Cups are full of five-petaled flowers. They are within a city with armed forces about, and the girl seems to be offering Cups of love to all who have enough sense to stop and appreciate what is being offered. The aspirant is looking to enjoy life here in this city, and you are seen here wandering along the streets in search of something. You need to be ever mindful of the beauty of Mother Nature. Even here in the city there can be found great love in abundance; keep an eye open for such beauty and generosity.

Blue Lace Agate

Blue Lace Agate has been corresponded to the Six of Cups. The Blue Lace Agate will lend its energy to help one be more tranquil and feel at peace. Carrying this stone will put the aspirant in touch with the inner beauty we all have within. When a Blue Lace Agate shows up in a reading, the aspirant is encouraged to relax and enjoy tranquility; the more the aspirant fights, the less likely they are to win. Try meditating on Blue Lace Agate. It may bring good fortune and peace of mind. Remember that every once in a while we need to let things be as they are. If you wish to alleviate a negative aspect from your life, you should seriously consider meditating with this stone. Contemplation of your troubles while holding this stone can help you find a solution to the problem.

VII - Seven of Cups

Seven of Cups
Blue Tiger Eye

The Seven of Cups depicts the choices that are before you, but do not lose focus of what is really important. Life is too short to dwell on making the wrong decision. Every day one is faced with decisions, how you act on those choices will influence the future. The aspirant should not be overly ambitious to receive the gifts of the Cups. The Seven of Cups hold many nice amenities, but things are not always what they seem. The aspirant has choices to make at this juncture on the Path. There are many, and the choice is yours, but you must choose wisely to learn the lessons of the dream.... Lessons that may bring great joy or distress, depending upon how you decide. In life, we all are riddled with choices on a daily basis and at any time we can make a mistake. A lot of decisions seem like they will lead to great joy but they inevitably fail in the long run, falling short of our expectations. Dreaming can be a nice way to escape the mundane everyday life, but stay there too long and you'll grow old and die without truly knowing what life is really about. We must remember to truly live life up until our moment of death. Do not let life pass you by just because you dwell in the past – live for today, dream of tomorrow, and learn from the past.

Blue Tiger Eye

Blue Tiger Eye has been connected to the Seven of Cups. These gray-blue shades of Tiger Eye are often referred to as "Hawks Eye". This is a stone that can be used to heighten one's psychic abilities. Use Blue Tiger Eye to psychically connect with another person who carries a similar stone. Meditating on Blue Tiger eye can help you to make the right choices. One's will must be strong to make it through challenging times. To move forward, try meditating on the issue with a Blue Tiger eye on your person. It can help chase away negative energies, leaving you peaceful and serene. One may also wish to carry this stone to promote good fortune. It may also assist in helping you make the right decisions for a favorable outcome.

VIII - Eight of Cups

Eight of Cups
Tanzanite

The person depicted here is leaving his Cups behind, along with his emotions and worldly possession in order to scale the mountain heights. The abyss does not appear to impede him; on the contrary it seems to move him forward on his Path towards greater achievement. There are times when we must learn what to leave behind so that we may have what we truly desire. The aspirant is on a journey to the heights of spirituality as depicted by the mountain peak. The abyss has been crossed, he needs only to keep moving and his travels will lead him to the summit. He has learned from his past endeavors and taken the precautions necessary to arrive safely at his destination. We are reminded to take up our tools and move ever forward; there are great times ahead for those who persist.

Tanzanite

Tanzanite has been assigned to the Eight of Cups. When Tanzanite appears in a layout, it is warning you to heed your emotional health. To find sanity in an insane world could be difficult to manage. Carrying the Tanzanite with you can help overcome loneliness and lift feelings of melancholy and depression. Pour your sorrows into the stone and then cleanse the stone to take them away. Get rid of the heartache and offer it up to Deity. They will take it from you and offer you peace in its place.

IX - Nine of Cups

Nine of Cups
Kyanite

A man sits with a happy smile upon his face. His worldly possessions are on a pedestal so all can see his achievements, but does he have everything? Material gain can only take you so far. If the Cups were to fall over their contents would be spilled and all gains lost. Be careful not to let the material things of this world take you from what is really important.

Kyanite

The Kyanite stone has been corresponded to the Nine of Cups. With this stone, it is possible to look into your inner-self to discover the truth of what you need in life. Be ever mindful of the Great Divine within. Kyanite brings understanding that worldly possessions are not all there is to life. Well-being is just as important, if not more so. Meditating on this stone will help to relieve stress. Make sure to implement regular cleansing of this stone.

X - Ten of Cups

Ten of Cups
Pink Pearls

Here the aspirant is surrounded by family with a nice house on a hill, a river running along the property, lush, fertile land, and a rainbow of Cups. The children are dancing and the couple hold their arms open in welcome to what they have. The rainbow holds a myriad of colors, as do the emotions. Keep in mind that emotions can change as quickly as the rainbow can disappear. This card indicates that should times get rough, your loved ones will be there to help you through it.

Pink Pearls

Pink Pearls have been connected to the Ten of Cups. You see the rainbow on the surface of this lustrous stone. The Pink Pearl brings tranquility and peace of mind when it is carried. When the Pink Pearl appears in a layout, it is revealing the loving and nurturing qualities that promote inner peace. While meditating upon this luxurious stone, remember the sea which it came from and the warm relaxing water which has the power to heal emotional pain. The Pearl cannot exist without the grain of sand. The rainbow is representative of perfection and the Pink Pearl can allow one to find love within. Self-love is very important when looking for love. This is not the same as self-centeredness. Spread love and watch it grow. Whether carrying or meditating on a Pink Pearl, remember to rid it of unwanted energies with regular cleansing.

Page of Cups

Page of Cups
Mother of Pearl

In this card the aspirant looks into his Cup only to find a fish looking back at him. There are no mountains in the background to scale, but behind the aspirant lies the abyss. How will the aspirant cross to the greater realm of spirituality? Will he even try? He seems to be preoccupied with the Cup and the fish. He may be lost at this time and his emotions are disturbed. The sea behind is rough and unsteady and in the distance looms the horizon. The aspirant would do well to get in charge of his emotions in order to get back on track.

Mother of Pearl or Nacre

Mother of Pearl, also known as Nacre, has been corresponded to the Page of Cups. When it comes into a reading, it is a signal that the emotional self is out of kilter. To right the emotions, one could carry the Mother of Pearl to utilize its energies. It has a calming effect on the possessor, the same tranquility found from gazing into the surf of the sea. Meditating on the Mother of Pearl can put you in a better mood and also bring out your creative side. When the aspirant wishes to rid the psyche of unwanted emotions, meditation with this stone will help banish them.

Knight of Cups

Knight of Cups
Apatite

The aspirant sits on the steed gazing into the Cup. The mountains stand on the other side of the river. He has the capacity to reach the distant mountains, but he chooses at this time not to pursue them. The aspirant must move forward, the mountains are waiting and only the effort is needed. To reach the heights, you'll need to throw off past emotions and take up the reins. While it is nice to dream, keep in mind that the Path to enlightenment awaits those who are willing to make the trek.

Apatite

The Apatite stone has been assigned to the Knight of Cups. The energies of this stone improve thought process. Meditation upon this stone will enhance ones mental faculties. By channeling the stone's energy through the solar plexus, it creates clear thinking and cuts through mental fog. When an Apatite appears, it is a sign that things are mellow for the time being. Sit back, relax, and enjoy the moment but try to do something creative. Apatite is excellent at inducing a creative environment.

Queen of Cups

Queen of Cups
Purple Aventurine

The Queen sits upon her throne on an island in the middle of the abyss. Surrounded by emotions, she holds a very delicate and decorated Cup balanced upon her hand. The mountain is seen here as a sheer-faced cliff on the opposite side of the abyss, one that is not easily scaled. The aspirant does not seem to want to move into action. Here the Queen sits in contemplation. Like the two court cards before her, she cherishes the revelry of her emotions. The cherubs upon her throne are mere people with the one on the bottom holding a fish. The aspirant is full of emotions at this time. Spending time to meditate on her emotions, she has stopped her journey. Here the Undines watch over the aspirant as she daydreams. She is not alone on her island, the sea dwellers are her constant companions. Continue along the Path and it shall lead you to great rewards. What awaits you is grander than can be expressed in words. Sometimes our emotions are too strong to overcome, and can be so potent that we do not want to deal with them. Though we may feel overwhelmed by emotions, we must keep going and not strand ourselves in seclusion. Bigger and brighter things are waiting further down the Path. Always remember we must be willing to fight for what is right. If you want to be happy, allow yourself to be so....only you have the power to do it.

Purple Aventurine

Purple Aventurine has been connected to the Queen of Cups. This stone helps calm the body and brings inner peace that gives us the ability to think creatively. Continued intimate contact with this stone will lead to the creative satisfaction of healing emotional wounds and disturbances. Meditation upon the Purple Aventurine will help to govern the forces of change. When this stone shows up, it is calling the aspirant forth to find inner peace. When one looks within, they will have emotional healing.

King of Cups

King of Cups
Spectrolite

This King sits upon his throne as if it floats on the world of emotions. The water is unsteady yet the King does not look worried, though his stone throne could sink at any moment. To the left is a white fish, and around the King's neck is a chain with a fish. In the King's right hand is the Chalice (the feminine), and in his left, the Scepter (the masculine). Once again the polarities are present. There are no enemies to be found in this card. The King's only enemy at this point is his emotions, which seem to be stormy; he may lose himself in them. The aspirant is warned to maintain emotional balance and not become overwhelmed to the point of anxiety.

Spectrolite

The Spectrolite has been attributed to the King of Cups. Strong, regal, and elusive in nature, these qualities are what make this stone so unique. Meditating on this stone will enlighten your mind to things that have been eluding you in the past. When in meditation, seek the illusions of your dreams to help find the answers to life's questions. What is it you wish to know? When a Spectrolite appears the aspirant is admonished to watch their emotional side, as it may be currently out of control. Carrying a piece of Spectrolite will help when you are over-worked and need to calm yourself. Relaxation is key at this time. Overworking, stress, and anger only lead to illness of the mind, body and spirit.

Chapter Eight: Minor Arcana
Pentacles: Earth

I - Ace of Pentacles

Ace of Pentacles
Rhodonite

The Path to the mountains are clearly marked, the archway to the future is before you. Take the Pentacle being offered, with love from the Great Divine. Use it to guide you along the Path to become the Hermit. The future awaits the wise one who takes up the tool and traverses the abyss to summit the mountain. The Divine is offering you a profound gift, a tool to help you achieve the goals one seeks. Learn the lessons offered to you by the suit of Pentacles. Do not tarry long in the valley, even though there is so much beauty there, the greater rewards are ahead of you. When one takes up the tool from the Divine, the journey starts; be prepared, the road is not easy to tread, though the rewards are greater than one could ever imagine.

Rhodonite

Rhodonite has been attributed to the Ace of Pentacles. Rhodonite provides grounding, improves self esteem, and helps the individual develop a healthy self-love. When a person is having great difficulty in self-forgiveness from past mistakes, Rhodonite promotes excellent healing; it is good for those who have a lot of stress in their lives. Rhodonite helps increase their inner strength and ability to stand up for themselves. When the Rhodonite appears in a layout, it may be alerting the aspirant that one's self esteem is not in balance, meditating on this stone will aid in balancing one's emotions. When Rhodonite comes up in the reading, it is a sign that the ego may need a little tweaking. You are encouraged to be aware of the instability in your life. The aspirant may need to revert back to the Ace of Pentacles when balance and grounding are needed.

II - Two of Pentacles

Two of Pentacles
Ocean Jasper

Here we see the aspirant juggling two Pentacles which he keeps moving in the continuous symbol of the infinity sign, while balancing on one foot. No mountains are visible on the horizon, only the choppy sea and ships in full sail that are trying to weather the storm. The aspirant is not moving towards the mountains or trying to cross the abyss; instead he is lost in the material world. The aspirant needs to keep in mind that to gain more, you must be willing to sacrifice what you have already gained. One's emotions are stormy at the moment and one may not see the approaching storm. The aspirant should set aside the material wealth of the day and focus on meditation; the grounding of the spirit will bring greater fortune to the aspirant. To keep what you have, keep your emotions in check so the things that you have achieved do not get swept away.

Ocean Jasper

Ocean Jasper has been corresponded with the Two of Pentacles. Ocean Jasper holds the energies of the ocean within its hardened shell. Like the tumultuous ocean, unbridled emotions lurk beneath the waves. The colors of this stone vary from spot to spot and each color pulls one deeper into the recesses of its inner folds. To unlock the Mysteries of this stone, one has only to exhibit Perfect Love and Perfect Trust. Carrying an Ocean Jasper around can calm inner turmoil and conflict within, and brings balance to the emotions to cease the storm. If the Ocean Jasper comes up in a layout, it is to show the aspirant that you may be trying to balance your emotions while juggling the material; a difficult thing to accomplish. To regain the sturdiness of solid ground and stop the emotional upheaval you must be willing to confront your emotions. Do not let your emotions carry you away.

III - Three of Pentacles

Three of Pentacles
Picture Jasper

Here we see the aspirant hard at work with many Pentacles around. The aspirant has gained much in notoriety with his skills and now works within the church as a servant of the faith. The monk, or priest, watches over the worker along with the lady counterpart to guide the aspirant in this endeavor. The aspirant patiently listens to them. If you are willing to do a good job, the rewards will be great. When one is faced with the work of the Divine, they should not chase the illusive dreams of a child, but stay rooted in the reality of the material world while remembering that money is not everything. Work hard, be kind, and live a spiritual life; the Great Divine is watching. The aspirant must keep in mind that even now as one works within their trade to fix the church, the Path will lead on to greater accomplishments. Now that the aspirant has gained the status which allows you to explore the far reaches of spirituality, the journey begins. Keep on the Path and learn the lessons of life so you may reach the summit of spiritual growth.

Picture Jasper

Picture Jasper has been assigned to the Three of Pentacles. Picture Jasper reminds one of the purpose and presence of Karma. Whether one does good or bad it creates a cosmic footprint. The aspirant could rewrite the Karmic influence by doing good deeds unconditionally, but the aspirant must be willing to do good without strings attached. Carrying Picture Jasper will put the aspirant in close contact with the energies needed to make a Karmic change. One thing that Jasper influences is the ability to affect one's personal energies, this would be useful in the practice of Magick. Meditation on this stone will help one to understand the finer aspects of Karma. Karma's effect is not inherently good nor bad, it is all reflected by one's perspective. When Picture Jasper makes itself known in a reading, it is telling the aspirant that a little hard work and dedication to helping out where needed will go a long way in the Karmic Records.

IV - Four of Pentacles

Four of Pentacles
Fancy Jasper

This person is contented with all they have and does not want to relinquish any of it. The city has brought the aspirant to where he is now, but he is out of touch with everyone around him. He sits away from all the other people of the city. The aspirant must learn to let go of the material so he may gain what is missing. In order to grab anything new, you must let go of what you already have hold of. Do not fret over setting things aside so you may obtain more. However, one should not be greedy lest it envelop you and destroy the spirit, causing you to lose all that has been gained. When you hold onto the material and forgo the spiritual side, the soul becomes lost and confused.

Fancy Jasper

Fancy Jasper has been attributed to the Four of Pentacles. When a Fancy Jasper appears in a layout, it may show that you are being over possessive. The aspirant is being admonished by this stone to stop and realize that there is more to life. When you carry this stone, it will lend its energies to help heal emotional hurts; you may feel lost and lonely at this juncture, but there is more happiness ahead. Keep on moving and look towards the future. Meditating on Fancy Jasper can illuminate the energies affecting your life. When the aspirant reaches the understanding of their emotions and realizes that life is not so bad, then the healing can commence.

V - Five of Pentacles

Five of Pentacles
Petrified Wood

The two people in this card seem to be leaving the church. The man is on crutches and the woman is barefoot. It is snowing outside and the stained glass window of the church is the only light. These people look hurt and deprived of the material fruition. To receive the material goods one needs to survive, it may be the time to ask for help if they need it; most likely they will receive the assistance they need. When one's needs are not being met, look toward the mountains for guidance. If you find yourself lost, hurt, or in need of assistance, look to the spiritual side.

Petrified Wood

Petrified Wood is honored to represent the Five of Pentacles. Strong and sturdy, Petrified Wood is older than humans and is considered to be a part of the realm of Tree Spirits and Dryads. Carrying a piece of Petrified Wood will help to improve one's mental and/or emotional stress. You can ground and center with a piece of Petrified Wood. Meditation on this stone will help alleviate stress. This stone can also help one to get what you most need. Help can come from unknown places so don't be afraid to ask for help. Keep your mind open to other possibilities that can help you achieve grand accomplishments. When Petrified Wood appears in a layout, it may be alerting the aspirant that hard times are coming. Perhaps the possibility of heartache, or even physical anguish might be near. Petrified Wood can relinquish copious amounts of Tree Spirit's energies to alleviate the stress and anger of everyday life. Find a little peace and tranquility in this stone's energies.

VI - Six of Pentacles

Six of Pentacles
Iolite

Here we have the aspirant helping others in need while holding the scales of balance; you have much to give and know that only through generosity will you truly have wealth. Though the aspirant is not looking to climb the heights at this time, they are pleased with the gifts of generosity and know that through kindness, respect, and love does one keep an even balance in life.

When someone becomes wealthy and is given the power that comes with it, they may become angry with those that do not have it. Do not let money overpower you. Help others when you can and you will have something even more valuable than gold – love, respect and peace of mind.

Iolite

The Iolite has been attributed to the Six of Pentacles. Iolite has the ability to conduct positive energy. This energy can be freely shared with others. Just be mindful to not give all you have or you'll be left drained, with nothing left over for yourself. Carrying an Iolite stone can help you project energies as well as attract them. Meditation upon this stone can help you understand how good it feels to live. When one feels depleted of energy you may draw upon this stone's forces to rejuvenate your vitality. Seek to refine your intentions. When you are enslaved by the mighty dollar, try to remember that money is not everything; you can't take it with you when you die and Karma can last forever.

VII - Seven of Pentacles

Seven of Pentacles
Tree Agate

The aspirant has obtained a fruitful harvest, one that is ready for picking. Having tilled the ground, watered and nurtured the plants, you now wait for the harvest time and may feel a bit sad that the end of the endeavor is near. Having succumbed to the rigors of labor, you may be contemplating what comes next. The mountains of spirituality rise behind the aspirant, and soon you will need to look towards the mountains to see that this harvest is not the end. In order to complete the journey you will have to reach down and harvest the crops. Gather the harvest and follow the Path to greater achievements.

Tree Agate

The Tree Agate has been corresponded with the Seven of Pentacles. Now that the harvest is at hand, you have the ability to count your blessings. The aspirant has achieved a harvest of material wealth, but what will you do with it now? The Tree Agate reveals the possibility of a greater reward. When carrying a Tree Agate, the aspirant is favored by the Devas, or plant spirits; it brings the possessor balance and grounding to the Earth Mother. Meditation with this stone will help you to make the right choices when faced with a dilemma. An in-depth meditation can delve deep into the psyche to reveal what troubles the aspirant. When the aspirant finds a Tree Agate in a layout, they might be reminded of the fact that even though the harvest is complete, winter awaits. If you are prepared for winter's hardships, you will not only survive it, you will produce an even greater harvest next year. Stow your seeds, keep them safe, and nurture your dreams. Now is the time to be thankful for all that you have.

VIII - Eight of Pentacles

Eight of Pentacles
Botswana Agate

The aspirant is hard at work to achieve what needs to be accomplished. You sit patiently doing what is necessary, but you do not look towards the mountains, nor to your dreams. Instead, you are rooted to the material gains of life. You may feel that through hard work you will get what you want in life, and that is true to a point – but you must embrace the spiritual disciplines to balance the Path. The aspirant has worked long and hard in this endeavor. Soon you may leave the workbench to sell the goods. The aspirant looks contented with the work. He is happy to do the job and do it well enough to make a profit. He must complete this task so he can reap the rewards and in this frame of mind he can do anything. Working hard at what you do and doing the best you can, will reap a great reward. Everyone needs money to survive, whether it is actually cash money or some material thing. Only through hard work can one learn the lessons of this card. If you work hard, you will achieve your goal. Moreover, combining your labors with the spiritual discipline of the Hermit may enable all your dreams to come true.

Botswana Agate

Botswana Agate has been assigned to the Eight of Pentacles. Botswana Agate can protect the wearer from negative influences and when you meditate on this stone it will strengthen your resolve to get the job done, as well as bringing peace, tranquility, and inner enlightenment. When a Botswana Agate appears in a reading, it may be alerting the aspirant that hard work and vigilance is needed at the moment. The material is needed to gain the things one needs but you should not always lean too heavily on them. Dependence on material wealth will only lead to the destruction of one's welfare. Be the owner of the material, do not let it own you.

IX - Nine of Pentacles

Nine of Pentacles
Morganite Beryl

The aspirant has quite the harvest, one you have been waiting for and now the fruits are ready to be gathered. The aspirant stands within the garden with a bird upon his finger. Material wealth is abundant, and he is quite pleased with the results – the aspirant is in control of life. The mountains are in the background still waiting to be climbed, but once again the aspirant is lost in the beauty of the here and now. There is nothing wrong with this but do not tarry long. Always be willing to move forward with the quest to fulfill your destiny. To complete this quest, one needs to be mindful that beautiful valleys are pleasant to behold, but the true quest is to reach the summit of spirituality; only then do we find true happiness and peace. The Path to greatness lies before you. Take heed to the call of Mother Nature, and keep looking towards the summit for answers to the intriguing questions at hand.

Morganite Beryl

Morganite Beryl has been attributed to the Nine of Pentacles. A Morganite stone is said to bring tranquility and inner peace. Meditation with this stone on the Heart Chakra will enhance the health of one's heart. Carrying a Morganite with you can add clarity to your motive and heighten your intuition. When a Morganite appears in a reading it should be interpreted as a good sign, for its latent energies can help to alleviate misconceptions about the material wealth one has, and guides you to the place you are destined to be The Hermit awaits you on the mountaintop.

X - Ten of Pentacles

Ten of Pentacles
Pipe-Stone

Here the aspirant sits contented in his old age among his family and friends. The aspirant has gained so much in life and there is no sign of discomfort or loss, only well-being. The Ten Pentacles are in the Kabbalistic Cross formation in the Tree of Life. This card shows the aspirant that family and well-being are important in this time of your life. Do not let material gain get in the way of the love of your friends and family. To achieve your goals you must work with your loved ones to gain tremendously in life. The aspirant is smart to keep in mind that there are much more rewarding things in life than the material world. When you keep your family close, the joy that is gained is fantastic.

Pipe-Stone

The Pipe-Stone comes to represent the Ten of Pentacles. Pipe-Stone helps to bring together family and friends. This stone can be carried to help alleviate tensions of family matters or bring two friends together. Meditation on this stone can allow the aspirant to reconcile differences with another person or help realize the problem in a situation. When a Pipe-Stone comes up in a reading, it may be alerting the aspirant to hidden troubles. One may wish to revert their attentions back to friends and family. Remember that friends are very important, but family should be even more so. To gain the stature of this elderly man, sitting amongst his loved ones, one must treat life as it is – precious!

Page of Pentacles

Page of Pentacles
Green Tourmaline

Here the aspirant holds the gains of the material while pondering the aspects of wealth. The fields lay tilled and ready for spring to come, but the aspirant is not looking towards them. Instead, the Page stands in the valley transfixed on what is already attained and not towards the future. The flowers are in full bloom and speak of the potential the aspirant has. You must let go of what you have in order to grasp other things. You must set aside the material to tend reality and implement your dreams into action. One can come to expect grand accomplishments if they learn the lessons the Page has to teach. One cannot go anywhere in the real world when they are burdened with the dreams that lie unfulfilled. In order to make your dreams come true, you need to step into reality. Do not hold your possessions too close to your heart or think that the world will stand still for anyone. Keep on the Path. There may be battles ahead, but the true test will be to get what you need in life and not just what you want Temper the ego, and let go of the material. Do not just sit there clutching your assets.

Green Tourmaline
Green Tourmaline has been connected to the Page of Pentacles. When the aspirant needs to be more self-confident in life, Green Tourmaline can help you complete your goals. Carrying a Green Tourmaline will protect against negative forces, as well as bring luck to the aspirant; an ideal stone for someone who may be embarking on a journey. Meditation on this stone can help you find the Path once more. When this stone appears in a layout, it is saying that the aspirant may be on a

journey or is about to start one. Either way, one must watch their step so as not to fall into the abyss. There is a possibility that negative forces are at work in your life. Now is not the time to slow down. The Green Tourmaline is telling the aspirant to move forward in order to attain the prize. When in doubt, revert back to the Ace of Pentacles to regain your bearings. Carrying this stone will dispel negative energies. When one
needs to be rid of these forces, meditation upon this stone can be beneficial.

Knight of Pentacles

Knight of Pentacles
Amazonite

This Knight holds in his hand a Pentacle as he contemplates what he has. He is so engrossed with his possessions that he no longer spurs the steed ahead into action. He no longer aspires to the heights of the mountains. Rather, he sits idly by with no determination or destination, with no desire to gain anything more than what he already has in his possession. The fields in the background have been tilled. Perhaps this Knight is not what he once was. Maybe he has just come from a battle, and now contemplates what he has left after the ordeal. The horse may just be resting now that the hard work of war is done. The smudges on his armor may be a surcoat. Is the branch on the horse's head an olive branch of peace? The aspirant should observe the full message of this card. Be careful of the idleness of the dream world and don't get caught daydreaming when there is work to be done.

Amazonite

Amazonite has been corresponded with the Knight of

Pentacles. With this stone comes great achievement. The aspirant has achieved an excellent stance atop the hill with the finery of the Knight. What more is there to gain? Carrying an Amazonite on one's person can help the aspirant to gain what is missing. This stone will help you to gain a better understanding of life's mysteries. When meditating with this stone you will find that only you have the power to make yourself happy. If an Amazonite shows up in a reading, you should not sit in wait; get up and do something. The only one who can make a change is you. Get up on the horse and charge into action now.

Queen of Pentacles

Queen of Pentacles
Green Aventurine

The Queen holds the Pentacle lovingly in her arms, as if it were a baby. Flowers surround the throne; these speak of abundance and motherly love. The mountains stand in the background as a symbol of the heights one can achieve. The wings on the Queen's crown speak of the flight of the mind. She looks as if she is contemplating some great mystery. Her wisdom is fathomless, her love for her people is unbound. She is loving and nurturing; she represents the community and she is rewarded highly within the hearts of her people. When the queen of Pentacles appears in a reading, it is a sign that there is an abundance of attainable goals. It doesn't matter whether you want or need something - it is okay to have nice things. This Queen teaches a valuable lesson here; if you are as loving and nurturing as a mother and care for others, then your deeds will not go unrewarded.

Green Aventurine

Green Aventurine has been attributed to the Queen of Pentacles. Green Aventurine can assist one to reach the heights of the mountains as well as rejuvenate the mind, body and spirit. This stone makes an intimate connection between the aspirant and the stone's energies when carried or meditated upon. A green Aventurine will lend its energies to alleviate stress, depression and create a sense of well-being. Meditation with this stone can improve one's creativity. When it appears in a reading, the aspirant might need to utilize the spiritual side to make things right. Spirituality can make miracles happen, but you have to belief in yourself first.

King of Pentacles

King of Pentacles
Chrysoprase

The King of Pentacles is surrounded by the things he had gained, with his scepter in one hand and his pentacle in the other. He still wears the armor of his last battle, ready to defend what he has or ready to go out and get more. The grapes tell of fertility of the kingdom and he will not allow anyone to take what is rightfully his. He has worked hard to gain this stature and notoriety, but his greed poses a risk to lose it all. The aspirant is warned not to relax too much, but to be ever vigilant and on guard lest you lose all you have worked for. The fruits of your labor only come to you with hard work and dedication. Go out and start up the quest once again. Find the Path to the mountains and search for the Hermit's light.

Chrysoprase

Chrysoprase has been assigned to the King of Pentacles. The Hermetic Principle, "As Above, So Below" is enclosed within this stone to delve deeper into the facets it holds, such as the ability to obtain the seat of nobility. You may not be a king, but you may feel like acting like one. Make sure you remember that nobility is regal, just, and kind. When meditating with this stone, the aspirant is advised to remember that even kings must lead with Perfect Love and Perfect Trust. When the aspirant carries this stone to utilize its qualities, you may find inner peace, serenity, and improved memory. When the Chrysoprase shows up in a reading, it is telling the aspirant that things will get better as the Chrysoprase is an omen of good things to come.

Chapter Ten: Acquiring Your Stones

Introduction to The Tarot-Stones was originally meant to come with complete sets of stones for this system, but it was decided to have the aspirant choose her or his own stones. A mailing list will be kept as we will be hoping to have complete sets available. [Contact The Hermit's Grove to be on the postal mailing list.] It is far easier to assemble one or two sets but quite complicated to have an offering at an advertised price for a complete set.

As you study the text, you will wish to begin acquiring a set of stones. This can be accomplished by either going to a store that sales gems and stones, or going online to the vast internet. The internet would be a good resource to find the best deals on the stones used in this system. While a gem and rock store will allow you to see the stones before you buy them. It wold be prudent to search for the best deals on a particular stone, and not let the glimmer of a beautiful stone blind you. A less glamorous road will get you to the same place just the same as the highway. Either way the wise shopper would need to know a few things to eliminate any complications so the price is not too high. The decision to buy expensive gems rather than the less pricey stones is inevitably up to the aspirant. The difference between faceted and tumbled stones will reduce the price dramatically and will not affect the energies of the stones. Another way to reduce the price is to choose wisely the gem quality. The gem quality is the rating of a gem's clarity, inclusions, and color. These do not affect the energies of the stone nor its virtues - only the price.

The size will also make a huge difference in price. One would not want the stone to be too small nor too big. The size should remain reasonable. Try to keep them between 4 millimeters to 12 millimeters. Any smaller and the stone may get lost.

The stones will be easer to identify if they are kept in a small zip lock bag with a slip of paper in each one to mark the stone's identity with the gem name and tarot card. 2" x 2" is a good size. 2" x 3" zip lock bags are easily found on amazon.com, for example. As this book goes to press you can purchase this size in quantities in the hundreds for under $10.00.

The bag can then be kept in a small cloth bag. The aspirant is well advised to become aware of the characteristics of each stone. Study the color, shape, and size of a particular stone. Be sure to ponder the stones completely, feel the energies that surrounds them. Form a relationship with each stone, for they will be your guides along the Path to greater comprehension and awareness. The objective is to become as aware of each stone as you would a person. This cannot be stressed enough. It is an important element to the success of this endeavor.

It would be wise to acquire a three-ring binder and plenty of paper. It is advisable to have both lined and unlined paper with the holes punched in order to fit the binder. The lined paper would be nice to write commentary and discoveries you make, and the blank paper could be used to draw diagrams/pictures on.

Once you develop an acquaintance with the stones be sure to cleanse them. Cleansing the stones might entail soaking them in water for a full lunar cycle. One could also place them in salt until all prior energies have been drained out leaving them clean and ready to use.

When using the Tarot-Stones your intuition should be your guide along the Path. Do not let a gut feeling go unheeded, it is usually the right choice. Do not hesitate to tote the stones around with you when you go out. How does carrying a certain stone make you feel? Does the feeling change when you switch to another stone?

If you feel compelled to replace an existing stone of higher worth what will you do with the replaced stone? Do not just discard it with the trash. It would be wise to put it in a special place. Perhaps you can bury it in a nice place in your gardens, or if you do not have a garden perhaps it would have a nice home in a nearby park. It might be a nice gesture to put it with a loved one that has passed over. Regardless of where you put discarded stone, make it special. The stone has touched your life so treat it kindly. When you show compassion and love to all creations that love is returned to you compounded.

Some Sources

The stones used in this book can be found through the internet, and can be found in a variety of grades.

Fire Mountain Gems and Beads, www.firemountaingems.com is a good source. Many of the stones can be purchase as beads at a modest price.

Rio Grande, riogrande.com is an exceptional source with quality stones both faceted and cabochons for making jewelry.

The Hermit's Grove, thehermitsgrove.org has a limited selection of stones. A price list can be obtained by writing to The Hermit's Grove, 16501 County 13, Houston, MN 55943. The Hermit's Grove is also the address to send information if you wish to be kept on a postal mailing list which will be used *only* to notify those interested if the author or publisher offers a complete set at a later date.

Great South Gems & Minerals, www.greatsouth.net has a large selection, primarily specimens.

Gems by mail.com, gemsbymail.com has wide range of faceted gemstones.

Although you may find stones on ebay.com, you may wish to be careful as some vendors sell stones which have been artificially colored. Be selective.

Bibliography

Rev. Paul V. Beyerl "Blessed is The Child of Light"-Fourth Edition- The Rowan Tree Church & The College of Mentors-Kirkland Washington 2001ce.

Rev. Paul V. Beyerl "A Wiccan Bardo, Revisited Revised Edition" The Hermit's Grove 1998ce.

Rev. Paul V. Beyerl- "Gem and Mineral Lore" First Edition- The Hermit's Grove Kirkland Washington 2005ce.

Rev. Paul V. Beyerl - "The Symbols of The Tarot First Edition-The Hermit's Grove- 2005ce.

Author Keith Ruch

On March 2nd 1973 a reincarnated soul entered the manifest world. Given the warrior name of Keith and the Hebrew surname of Ruch, (pronounced ROOK) Keith has struggled through a life of mental illness. He has fought diligently to overcome his problems and through proper medication and counseling he has persevered. Keith is compassionate, understanding, and giving. He is outgoing with a kind, generous nature that helps out people in need. A charismatic, intuitive lover of knowledge, Keith is a role model and a positive influence for others who take the time to listen.

In 2002 Keith Joined the Prisoner Outreach Program, studying under Rev. Paul Beyerl and the Rowan Tree Church. Over the years he completed those studies and became a Member of The Rowan Tree Church. He is a Lay Minister and has served on the Board of Directors of The Rowan Tree as well as being a contributing author to The Unicorn newsletter.

Keith was in search of a teacher to guide the way to the summits of higher understanding, but the Charge of the Goddess says," That if which thou seekest thou finest naught within thee thou shalt never find it without thee." The teacher Keith was searching for was within himself.